C000021543

Let's program a PLC
First step in
TIA Portal V15_1

Automatic sliding gate
Vol. 1

first edition 2020

The simplest and clearest introduction available in the bibliography not only for immediate application, but also for what is required by higher educational programs, university programs, and business areas.

Written, edited and published

By

Eng. Prof. Dott. Marco Gottardo PhD

"Let's program a PLC, First step in TIA Portal V15"

Automatic sliding gate Vol.1

First edition © **Marco Gottardo 2020**

This edition was edited and published in September 2019 by Marco Gottardo.
All rights reserved. No part of this publication may be reproduced, stored in a storage system or transmitted in any form or by any means, mechanical or electronic, without the written permission of:

Marco Gottardo, C.F. GTTMRC68R06G224I,
Via Colombo 14, 30030 Vigonovo (VE) Italia.
E-mail: ad.noctis@gmail.com

ISBN-13: 9781688793187

Index:

Preface to the first international Edition:

This book is the first international edition of industrial automation series by the teacher eng. Marco Gottardo.

The contents respond to the need for clarity and synthesis requested by the students in training courses, bacherlor and engineering, bringing together international technicians in a common language and modus operadi.

Designed for self-taught students, it prefers the practical example to the theoretical explanation.

It makes the new technician autonomous in the development of small and medium-sized industrial plants.

 Starting from the year 2019 it is one of the texts officially adopted for professional training courses organized by G-Tronic Robotics based in the Industrial Area of Padua.

The lessons are accessible for students from all over the world in English.

The G-Tronic training center offers accommodation. Lessons need a full immersion week.

To obtain information or date your training period, simply write to the email ad.noctis@gmail.com

The book contains the first essential steps for using the TIA PORTAL V15_1 platform.

The projects are presented in increasing order of difficulty and each topic is immediately usable in the workplace.

The book is followed by three other volumes, advanced PLC programming, programming exercises, professional PLC programming oriented to industrial processes study.

Marco Gottardo.

Dott. eng. PhD Marco Gottardo.

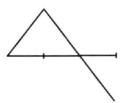

Quote, "The razor":

The solution that appears simpler is often also the right one.

Frustra fit per plura quod fieri potest per pauciora

Guglielmo of Occam.

Work in progress

1. The automatic sliding gate. (this publication, Venezia, late 2019).

2. Elevator installed in a three-floors building. (next edition early 2020)

3. Sun Tracker photovoltaic panel. (next edition early 2020)

4. Sequence generator and combinatorial logic. (next edition middle 2020)

5. Analog signal, handly and normalization. (next edition late 2020)

6. Inverters and three-phase asynchronous motors. (date not yet released)

7. Closed loop control. (date not yet released)

8. Data exchange and communication. (date not yet released)

9. Experiments with encoder, axis control, motion control. (date not yet released)

10. SCADA. (date not yet released)

11. PLC programming exercises and final tests

12. Other publications not yet planned.

The titles indicated are part of the series for industrial automation international educational:

Let's program a PLC First step in TIA Portal V15_1

Vol. 1

The yellow "G-T", on the cover, it is a G-Tronic Robotics Logo, the Marco Gottardo company. It can't be used without the written permission of:

Marco Gottardo, C.F. GTTMRC68R06G224I,
Via Colombo 14, 30030 Vigonovo (VE) Italia.
E-mail: ad.noctis@gmail.com

To the left: Ravi Shankar Munganda, , student, India
To the right: Marco Gottardo, teacher, Venice, Italy,

Preface

Any control system can be implemented in two ways, in wired logic or in programmable logic.
The wired logic is achieved by connecting individual elements such as sensors of various kinds, buttons, switches, photocells, or relay coils, etc.
The signals paths along the wiring constitute the program of the wired logic.

Any change or modification of the program would involve wiring the electrical structure.

Therefore, operating in wired logic is useful only when you are absolutely certain that the system to be built is in its final version and also should not be subjected to periodic calibrations for production changes, furthermore the cycle is limited to a few movements because otherwise the electrical components to be used increase exponentially.

The programmable logic offers a high degree of standardization in electrical connections, in fact these will depend only minimally on the application thanks to the role played by the software contained in the memory of a 32-bit microcontroller, for example Infineon, microchip, AVR, Freescale, which represents the brain of the programmable controller and that resides in the logical unit improperly called CPU.

The purpose of the book is to introduce students to the programming of particular programmable devices called P.L.C. (programmable logic controller) whose central component is a microcontroller capable of managing I/O expansions connected to the bus.

The program to be executed by the programmable controller is loaded into the program memory by means of a special programming device, called PG, now it can be replaced by a normal PC typically connectable via Ethernet connector using the protocol that Siemens calls PN for extended Profinet, evolution of industrial ethernet.

The program specifies the sequence and conditions according to which the control actions must be performed by P.L.C.

The signal generators, today called sensors and transducers, most commonly connected to a programmable device are: Button contacts, limit switches, pressure switches, thermometers, but also devices that contain a microprocessor (intelligent sensors) and communicate via serial protocols, often ASi (AS-Interface), EtherCAT (Ethernet Control Automation Technology), or even based on TCP/IP.

If a modification to the program is necessary, it will not be essential to rewire the hardware circuitry, but it will be sufficient to connect with the appropriate programming device and change the logic in software networks.

In recent years, the technology of industrial automation has been reoriented by the classic stand alone systems, composed of a machine with its own electrical control panel with PLC and relative field-oriented program, or field distributed systems in which a single central unit interconnects and it controls the decentralized peripherals, often using the protocols mentioned above or simply as an extension of the Bus.

Today, the PLCs of various manufacturers, including Siemens, seek to converge towards a standardization of languages, architectures and operating methods, in order to facilitate migrations from a different brand and model. What seems more a normative imposition rather than a coherent choice from manufacturers is summarized in IEC 61131-3, whose third revision, currently in use, dates back to February 2013.

The first normalization concerns software languages which according to IEC 61131-3 can be represented in 5 ways:

- **Ladder diagram** (LD), graphic language divided into segments formed by horizontal uprights and vertical power lines. The name derives from the English Ladder, a folding staircase, whose structure recalls the shape. Developed to benefit electrical and electromechanical extraction programmers.

- **Function block diagram** (FBD), graphic language, in which the functions are roughly electronic symbols, including the known basic logic gates, developed to benefit electronic extraction programmers.

- **Structured text** (ST), textual language, divided into 4 columns, jump labels, operation, operand, comment. It vaguely remembers an assembly, familiar to the electronic programmers of old molds, tends to fall into disuse although it is a very powerful and complete language. It is not present in the S7-1200 series.

- **Instruction list** (IL), Textual language, of Pascal derivation, foreseen by the IEC61131-3 standard, will be present in every new generation PLC. Very familiar to computer programmers.

- **Sequential function chart** (SFC), Basically it is the Grafcet, it organizes the program in sequential or parallel sequential sections. Very useful in certain types of cyclical process but highly limiting in the average of cases, for this reason it is not widely used. An example has been given in the first part of the text.

Since the normalization imposes a strong internationality the German disappears as default setting and the English appears also in the Siemens productions. Students and new technicians are advised to set the TIA interface, in the portal view, in English. After a small initial difficulty there will be great advantages especially in the increasingly stringent need to work in sites located abroad and to communicate in technical language with colleagues and operators of a different nationality. (ex. E ->% I, A ->% Q, etc).

The P.L.C. is an expandable modular machine the main components are:

- The processor (CPU block)
- Memory (inside the CPU block, today often also in SD)
- I / O cards (input / output expansion blocks)
- The Bus system (allows the connection of blocks in the same rail or different)
- The power supply (called PS, Power supply, almost always at 24V D.C.)
- The decentralized field devices (ET200, SLIO, WAGO, MURR, Weidmuller, etc.)
- Actuators and Servo drives, (drive devices for MAT and Brushless)
- PLC firmware operating system, not erasable from the CPU unit.
- The operating system mentioned in the last point is a fundamental component of the controller and determines its operation at startup and in its cyclic execution state.

It is the **IEC 61131-3** standard that regulates its algorithmic functionality and is a fundamental step that the technician must know.

When the PLC switches, on command, from the STOP situation to the RUN situation, a standardized initialization process takes place. First of all, a non-cyclical organizational block is evoked and launched in all Siemens models, with the purpose of initializing the system and checking the machine zero point. Siemens has established the OB100 block for this purpose.

At the end of the single scan / execution of the content that we will put in OB100, the control is passed to the cyclic organization block OB1, which creates the main loop.

This loop can be interrupted by events that occur on the machine or in the software (for example in diagnostics or communications) through the automatic evocation of other organizational blocks called interrupt OBs.

The execution then passes to the functions (and to the functionals, that is premature to further investigate here), which at any time may be interrupted by the action of opportune organizational blocks OB, timed, of event interrupts, diagnostics, etc.

In essence, a PLC, although an industrial type and certified to work in these hostile environments (it cannot be made by an embedded system with a microcontroller such as Atmel), it is always a computer and therefore the basic rules of information technology remain valid .

The most basic is that the functions must be parameterizable, so calls must be able to pass variables. It must be possible to pass these variables by copy or by address, therefore the pointers must exist, there must be dedicated "protected" memory areas to store the instances (input data set) of the calls to the functions themselves.

Historically, in computer science there was a differentiation between procedures and functions (think of the archaic Pascal today), the concept remains valid and therefore we could define in our PLC functions of type FC and functional type FB, whose difference to the beginner can be obscure and will be clarified between the pages of the text.

In the new Siemens PLC, series 1200 and 1500, the standard communication protocol is the Profinet.
The cable to be used is the RJ45 type, and the ports will be able to automatically recognize if it is a Patch or cross configuration.
The color assigned to this standard is green.
Today even in the simplest plant there will be a human to machine interface, called HMI.
For this reason, each project starts by setting up the communication network and assigning the IP addresses to the components taken from the hardware catalog.

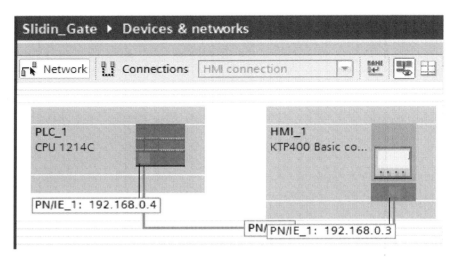

How a PLC operates according to IEC 61131-3.

The elaboration of a program by a PLC is cyclical and constrained to a sequence that, in a first approximation, makes it blind for half of the time in which it is active.

For this reason we cannot use a normal digital input to acquire a fast signal whose frequency is not at least half (better if still lower) than the cyclical processing frequency, as required by Shannon's rule.

The PLC on power-up and at the Stop / RUN transition, resets all the internal memory, obviously excluding the area where the program is resident. This guarantees that in the first scan cycle (unless otherwise pre-set by the programmer) we will find all the timers, counters, markers and I/O to zero.

Generally speaking, the PLC does not look directly at the field, but its image acquired from the input terminals and stored in a special area of the internal memory that Siemens calls in the previous versions, in German PAE, today thanks to IEC known as IPI (input peripherals images) or process image of the inputs.

During the acquisition and update phase of the IPI (or PAE) the PLC outputs are frozen in the state imposed in the previous cycle.

At the end of the scan of the input terminal blocks, these are frozen so any fast / impulsive signal is ignored, at the end of having no ambiguity in the analysis of the IPI (PAE) and the passage of this process area in the form of a Boolean matrix in memory.

The elaboration involves the extrapolation of a process image of the outputs represented by a matrix of booleans organized in bytes of memory, that Siemens calls in German PAA known thanks to the IE as IPO or IPU, (process image of the outputs).

Only at the end of the PAA (IPU) outpus are unlocked on which this matrix is copied, updating the output terminals, byte by byte.

Once updated, the outputs are frozen in this state and the cycle is repeated for as long as the program is running.

> It is therefore clear that for 50% of its life the PLC is blind with respect to the signals at the inputs because it is involved in updating the output terminal blocks.

This procedure more than a disadvantage due to the inevitable delays is a guarantee of stability of execution.

The problem of fast signals coming from the field such as an encoder remains. You will have to use a hardware counter, in technical bibliography known as HSC, (Higt speed counter), which once configured, typically by means of "pre-packaged" program blocks that require parameters, will launch an interrupt signal at a height reached. In essence it is the hardware that keeps the axes of the automaton and not the normal cyclic execution.

Similarly, there is dedicated hardware for sending and receiving communication packets in industrial network protocols such as Profibus, industrial ethernet, Profinet, Ethercat, ModBus, etc. These blocks are called by Siemens "communication coprocessors" indicated briefly with the abbreviation CP.

The above, also in relation to the cyclical nature of the program, is not in contrast with the normal division into blocks of Step 7 and its organization in references and jumps.

Before entering in cyclic execution, the program executes a code block in a non-sequential way, useful for machine setup and communication and peripheral diagnostics.
For Siemens products this block is called OB100.

Standard memory addressing

The Siemens PLCs adapt to the IEC addressing of the locations by first enumerating the Byte and then the Bit to accessed in the read or write mode.
To make the Siemens data areas compatible with the IEC standard, it is necessary to disable the optimized access in Siemens mode. This makes the TIA Portal environment compatible and everything that concerns non-Siemens products.
The data is stored in the areas indicated with the abbreviation DB.
The DBs are uniquely numbered so as not to create conflict during the execution of the program.

DB10.DBX 0.0 ->Access to the zero bit of the zero byte of the data block number 10.

Integer numbers require 16 consecutive bits, these space is known as "word". Only the access point must be specified to access these locations.
it is also a good idea that every integer data is allocated with access points of even address.

DB2.DBW 4 -> Access the integer that starts at bit 5.0 and ends at bit 4.7, two bytes are committed.
In analogy we can access the real numbers, which involves 32 bits, or 2 words, or 4 bytes. The offset must be taken into account in order not to create a conflict or an overlap in the data.
DB2.DBD 6 -> commits 4 bytes starting from the sixth.

Fundamental concepts: The zero Machine position.

Let's consider a mechanical structure, who the dimensions are not important, and the automation must be resolved using a PLC.

A particular position, generally chosen by the designer of the structure in a manner consistent with the sequence to be performed, and the present mechanical constraints, imposes on the control system a specific condition of the matrices of IPI (PAE) and IPO (PAA), in others words a particular condition of ones and zeros both in input and in output.

This condition is called zero machine or home position, and is the starting point for the cyclical evolution of the program.

If a system is not set to zero point, the cycle cannot be simulated with the appropriate tools, for example PLCsim, also available for S7-1200 models from the CPU firmware version 4.0 or upwards, because the correct start-up situation of the captive.

PLCsim cannot simulate program in a CPU running firmware 31 or 30.

The three main types of automation are:

- A system is called manual if from the zero machine position, it transitions from one stable state to another, until it returns to zero machine only with the consent of the operator.
- A system is said to be semiautomatic if from the zero machine position, received an operator consent, it executes a sequence of transitions between stable states until it returns to zero machine. Here awaits a new consent from the operator.
- A system is said to be automatic when from the position of zero machine it receives a first consent of the operator that allows it not only to transit from a stable state to the next, but also to cross the zero mschine condition for a predefined number of times or even in Infinity loop .

An intuitive example of a domotic gate.

Although this automation is not normally implemented with a PLC, it is a milestone in automation courses thanks to the familiarity of the cycle that follows, known to all.

His zero machine position will be:

Input state at zero machine (IPI)		Output state at zero machine (IPO)	
Pushbutton or opening consent	0	Contactor motor open gate	0
Limit switch gate open	1	Contactor motor close gate	0
Limit switch gate close	0	Yellow blinking lamp	0
Overall photocell	1		
Pneumatic edge* UNI 8612 1	1		

* For pneumatic edge, pneumatic safety decice UNI 8612, is meant a safety device, which has the appearance of a soft rubber edge, which typically hides one or more end stops. It is mounted on the side of the movement, in this case in the vertical part of the sliding gate leaf, with the aim of blocking the opening in the event that an obstacle, for example a child, is in the sliding rail. At zero machine the signal is present due to intrinsic safety issues, in fact if the wire is broken the signal to the PLC is interpreted as a safety intervention.

In the simulation phase, before clicking on the RUN command of the simulator we should set up the virtual inputs and outputs as per the table indicated above, specific to each single problem.

If we do not follow these instructions, even a correct program may be incorrect or not run by the simulator.

In the next image an example of pneumatic edge.

Sensing edges respond to obstructions in openings controlled by garage doors, rolling doors, rolling grilles or gates and signal motor operators.

These edge devices are usually attached to, or are part of, the bottom edge of an upward acting door or grille - or a leading and/or trailing edge of a horizontally moving gate.
Activation of a sensing edge will cause the motor operator to perform one of three different actions on the door/grille/gate:

     1. stop during either a closing or an opening movement,
     2. stop and open during a closing movement, or
     3. prevent a closing action from an open position.

To ensure safe operation of the door/grille/gate, the electric air switch should be adjusted to the highest sensitivity that is practical.

If the tube is cut open or an end plug falls out, the sensing edge may not function properly.

In order to prolong the life and effectiveness of the sensing edge, the tube inside the pneumatic sensing astragal should not be compressed when the door/grille/gate is closed.

The CPU "sees" the outside world through the terminal boards of the input boards, it queries the status of the inputs by checking whether the voltage signal is present or not. Unless otherwise specified, the digital levels are 0 - 24V DC.

The CPU always manages the output expansion cards supplying voltage with 0 -24 DC levels, the standard of which is 0.5 A current flow rate per transistor, on the connectors of the connectors according to the input processing set by the program.

In any case the PLCs guarantee the galvanic separation both in input and in output, otherwise they would not pass the necessary CE certification by the manufacturer.

Output expansions can be transistor or relay type. In the second case it will be possible to directly drive alternating loads with the obvious power limitations due to the capacity of the internal contacts, for example we could drive the contactor coils in 24AC, but not the armature of a three-phase asynchronous motor.

In the case of heavy loads it is in fact used to control a servo relay with the PLC, which in turn drives a powerful contactor with reinforced contacts, typically with three parallel paths for the three phases U, V, W, which will take care of driving the induced by a powerful AC motor.

These remote switches always have auxiliary contacts in which to carry a continuous 24V voltage to be closed in appropriate PLC inputs so that the effective closure or mechanical opening of the contacts can be tested by software, then a feedback control.
In general, when it is necessary to drive outputs with rapid repetitions, in DC, with 0-24V standard we will use the transistor outputs, when instead we have to drive more heavy and even bipolar electric loads we will use the galvanic separation offered by the use of an internal relay or external to the expansion card.

Even in the case of transistor outputs we will not be able to generate frequency commands greater than the cyclical times of the PLC, as we can test by driving a transistor output with the denied of itself. We will note that we will hardly exceed kHz even with the latest generation of PLCs. The S7-300 family will give us about 500Hz.

The PLC's bus system.

The Bus system is a set of internal connections for the transmission and exchange of signals, the PLCs normally organize the Buses in Bytes even if the central processor has a 32bit architecture.
The Bus is divided into three main parts:

- Address bus (to access the addresses of the individual bytes per byte).
- Data bus (to read data from input cards or send them to 8.16.3bit output data).
- Command bus (to manage control and command signals from P.L.C. to the field).

Of fundamental importance is the power supply, it provides not only the power supply to the microcontroller which is inside the CPU block (5 Volt) to supply the voltage for the signal generators (sensors) and other devices connected to the board's I /O, generally according to the industrial standard at 24VDC. Today, in Field oriented systems, decentralized peripherals mount local power supplies in the first slots of the ET200, SLIO VIPA, WAGO, MURR, Weidmuller, Devicenet etc. terminal blocks

The P.L.C. it is able to process both digital and analog type signals.

Unless otherwise indicated, Siemens uses 12bit analogue digital converters, with 0 - 10V voltages, but through software settings, or hardware where it is possible to operate on dip switches or switches, it will be possible to acquire the industrial standard 4-20mA, or the bipolar - 5V - + 5V, or other standards, for example 0-10mA, for which we refer to the manual of the specific models.

The outputs can also be analogue and are widely used to control actuations, for three-phase motors, (inverters), in order to generate a proportional frequency. There are more extensive explanations in the text.

For analogue signals we will discover the importance of the integer **27648**, as a full-scale of the ADCs regardless of the bit resolution.

In general, all new PLCs have I/O points with functions or even addresses that can be remapped, in the sense that it is possible to assign via software or hardware an input or output address that is more convenient for us, for example because we are converting a old S5 series archaic program, or from the next S7-300 in order to make it work in a new S7-1500 or S7-1200 controller.

It must be said that as of today, February 2018, the S7-300 series PLCs are still for sale, as are the VIPA Speed7 compatible ones, and can be programmed with the new TIA Portal V14 SP1 version.

A wide selection of CPUs 300 and 400 can be found in the hardware catalog section of the TIA Portal V15 platform and can be configured in mixed networks together with the S7-1500 and S7-1200, making it possible to expand existing systems without proceeding with the scrapping of the already installed panels and electrical cabinets.

Even areas of retention (retentive) memory, that is able to remember the previous state after the loss of voltage or interruption of the program, can be relocated where it makes us more comfortable releasing ourselves from the fixed positions that the S100-U series required, for example of the archaic Step5.

It must be said that for the reading of so-called "fast" signals we must not rely on the standard I / O pins, but on the fast counting inputs, equipped with dedicated hardware that does not follow the cyclic processing times but generates a special signal of interrupt.

This applies to both inputs (encoders) and outputs (PWM generators, pulse width modulation and PTO pulse train output) useful for generating commands to be sent to servo drives for brushless motors.
The modern decentralized peripherals allow to reach the point of concentration of the signals with a single Profinet cable, considerably reducing costs.

The addresses of the inputs and outputs in these devices are seen as if they were on the central CPU. The use of Profinet commands is not necessary.

Introduction: The TIA Portal V15_1 environment

On 27 December 2017 the TIA V15 version was launched on the market, on which this book is based.
Until today, in september 2019, it is the last released by Siemens.
The TIA Portal, in its basic philosophy, wants to integrate, in a single platform, tools of various kinds, for example the programming of PLC models previously kept separate as well as the design of supervision on HMI (human machine interface) and systems in rapid evolution called SCADA.

At the same time as the Step7 package, integrated into the TIA Portal, at least the license manager software will always be installed.

Also the V15 version, has some incompatibilities with the Windows10 software, and may require the application of the compatibility with Windows 7 to the main DLLs.

To identify the DLLs, simply execute the right button on the license manager icon, on the desktop, and on properties, search the file path.

Once you identify the location, operate on the properties and apply Windows 7 compatibility, for all users.

The interface of the V15 version is practically identical to the V14 version, the most widespread also in 2018.

This allows programming of the Simatic S7-300 systems, S7-400, S71200, S7-1500, WinAC, and integrating a basic version of WinCC allows programming of the main operating panels of type KTP and OP.

The additional packages installation allows to expand the functions of WinCC to more advanced and performing operator panels.

In case of development and release of new hardware products, SIEMENS provides additional packages named HSP, acronimus of Hardware Support Package.

A good installation of TIA Portal should integrate at least, Step 7 professional, WinCC Comfort or Advanced, Start Drive also known as Motion control.

The environment have two operation mode, the portal view, with web setting, and the project view.

in the Portal view we set the project name and select the hardware components. We set up the Profinet network and assign IP addresses.

The project view is more useful for using the editors for both Step 7 and WinCC.

Within project view there is a subdivision into 3 plus 2 windows. The first three are the work areas, the second are the system areas, they provide operational information and the dialogue with the compiler.

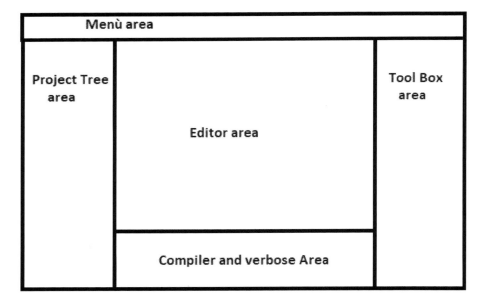

Window splitting is common to every modern programming platform in high-level languages, such as Eclipse or Visual studio.

Compiling the code before downloading is essential. It can be local to the point where we changed or global. In this case, right-click on the station icon where we want to act. Compile hardware and software.
If we forget to compile a part of the source an error is returned and the download is blocked.

Step 7 program blocks

A Step 7 program is divided into 4 types of blocks, with specific functions.

The simplest program consists of at least one cyclic executive, a function called and a data area in which to insert the variable to exchange with the HMI interface.

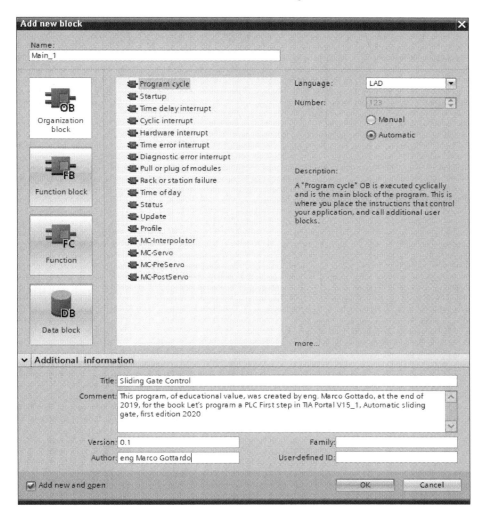

The block types are:

- OB -> Organization blocks as in the image they have preassigned purposes.
- FB -> when the code can be reused, the parameterization takes place in the instance DB.
- FC -> functions that mainly use global variables
- DB -> container of exchange variables between HMI and CPU.

The initial sequence set by the PLC operating system activates OB100, for a non-cyclic sequential execution.

It is used for system setup, for checking initial values, for mechanical status, etc.

OB1: A "Program cycle" OB is executed cyclically and is the main block of the program. This is where you place the instructions that control your application, and call additional user blocks.

OB100: A "Startup" OB will execute one time when the operating mode of the PLC changes from STOP to RUN. After completion, the main "Program cycle" OB will begin executing.

OB20: A "Time delay interrupt" OB will interrupt cyclic program execution when a specified delay time has expired. The delay time is specified in the input parameter of the extended instruction "SRT_DINT".

OB30: A "Cyclic interrupt" OB allows you to start programs at periodic intervals, independently of cyclic program execution. The intervals can be defined in this dialog or in the properties of the OB.

OB40: A "Hardware interrupt" OB will interrupt cyclic program execution in reaction to a signal from a hardware event. The events must be defined in the properties of the configured hardware.

OB80: A "Time error interrupt" OB will interrupt cyclic program execution if the maximum cycle time has been exceeded. The maximum cycle time is defined in the properties of the CPU.

OB82: A "Diagnostic error interrupt" OB will interrupt cyclic program execution if a diagnostics-capable module, for which the diagnostic error interrupt has been enabled, recognizes an error.

OB83: A pull or plug OB is called after removing or inserting a configured module.

OB86: A pull or plug OB is called after removing or inserting a configured module.

OB10: Time-of-day OBs are started either once at a specific time or periodically.

OB55: The operating system calls the status interrupt OB when it receives a status interrupt. This can happen if the module of a slave changes its operating mode.

OB56: The operating system calls the update interrupt OB when it receives a update interrupt. This can happen if you modify the parameters at a slot for a slave or device.

OB57: The operating system calls the OB for manufacturer-specific or profile-specific interrupts
when it receives a manufacturer-specific or profile-specific interrupt.

OB92: The organization block MC-Interpolator [OB 92] is used to prepare and monitor setpoint values in Motion Control.
It is started by the system every time the OB MC-Servo is executed.

OB91: The organization block MC-Servo [OB 91] is used for Motion Control functions such as I/O access, signs of life and position control.

OB67: The organization block MC-PreServo [OB 67] is called immediately before the MC-Servo OB.

OB95: The organization block MC-PostServo [OB 95] is called immediately after the MC-Servo OB.

Fundamental concept.

The initial sequence set by the PLC operating system activates OB100, for a non-cyclic sequential execution.
It is used for system setup, for checking initial values, for mechanical status, etc.

The standard sequence of a minimum program for Siemens PLCs shows this block structure.

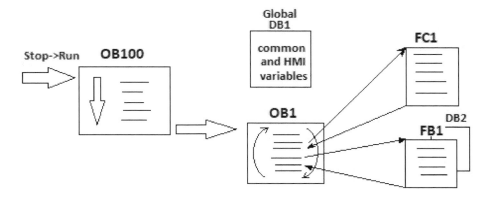

Note that the block named FB1 is combined with a particular data block, here numbered DB2.

For the moment let's just say that this is the instance DB of the parameterized function FB1 and that it contains the global exchange variables defined in the calling block.

what is an global DB?

One of the basic concepts of step 7 programming concerns the use of global data blocks.
There are two types of data areas, the global data blocks, accessible by all and the data blocks associated with data exchange between a function block and the main program.
To add a global data block, useful for linking variables, called tags, to an HMI panel, click on Add new block and insert as shown in the figure.

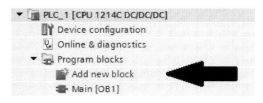

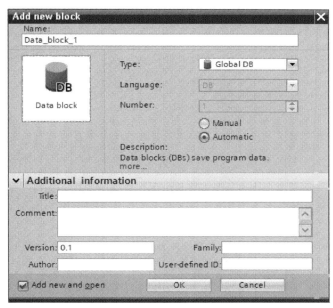

Confirming the command the DataBlock appears in the project tree and is ready to be populated with the HMI to CPU exchange variables and between CPU and HMI.

To rename the data block you have to act on F2.

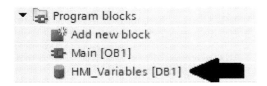

It is important that the variables have a name that recalls the connection with the HMI device.
The suffixes HMI_ variable_name or TP_variable_name are the most suitable.

For example, enter the minimum commands useful for controlling and monitoring the domotic gate.

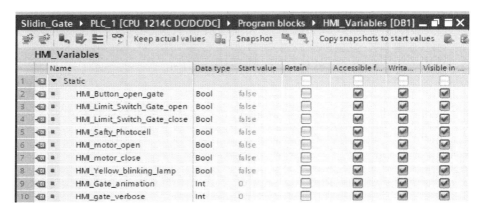

		Name	Data type	Start value	Retain	Accessible f...	Writa...	Visible in ...
1		▼ Static			☐	☐	☐	☐
2	■	HMI_Button_open_gate	Bool	false	☐	☑	☑	☑
3	■	HMI_Limit_Switch_Gate_open	Bool	false	☐	☑	☑	☑
4	■	HMI_Limit_Switch_Gate_close	Bool	false	☐	☑	☑	☑
5	■	HMI_Safty_Photocell	Bool	false	☐	☑	☑	☑
6	■	HMI_motor_open	Bool	false	☐	☑	☑	☑
7	■	HMI_motor_close	Bool	false	☐	☑	☑	☑
8	■	HMI_Yellow_blinking_lamp	Bool	false	☐	☑	☑	☑
9	■	HMI_Gate_animation	Int	0	☐	☑	☑	☑
10	■	HMI_gate_verbose	Int	0	☐	☑	☑	☑

In principle, Boolean type variables must be defined when buttons, switches or pilot lights are turned on from the touch panel.

When numerical or proportional fields are piloted, integer or real variables must be declared.

The string variables will be used for the fields "text list", like will show later.
These can represent warnings or alarms or process status or mechanical positions, in example "gate is open".

The insertion of a button takes place through the menu "Elements". Just drag the icon onto the graphic area of the HMI screen.

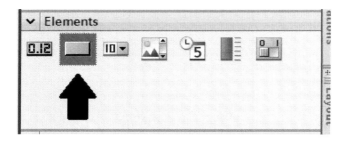

if you need to access the DB variables from a non-Siemens operator panel, you must disable the optimized access by removing the check box from the block properties.

Connect the HMI variables to the global DB

Always connect the buttons and graphic elements to the global DB variables, even if WinCC offers the touch panel variables.
Navigate on the project tree using the 3 dots browser until you reach the global DB on the CPU station, in the project tree.

Change the text contained in the button by simply clicking the inside and changing the label.

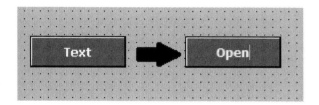

Select the renamed button and under the Tab "Properties", select "Events".
Appear list of possible events that can be triggered by the button.

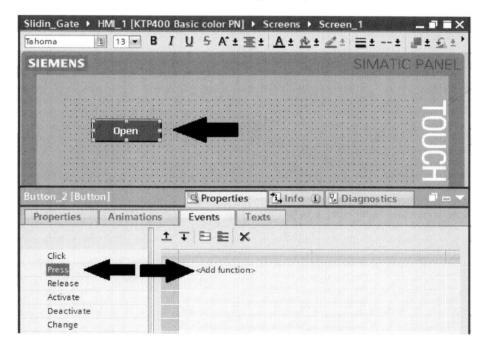

The simplest and most effective configuration for a monostable button is the Press and Release sequence.

When pressed, the button must set a bit at the end of the global DB on the CPU.
When the button is released, the same bit must be reset.

The simplest and most effective configuration for a monostable button is the Press and Release sequence.

When pressed, the button must set a bit at the end of the global DB on the CPU.

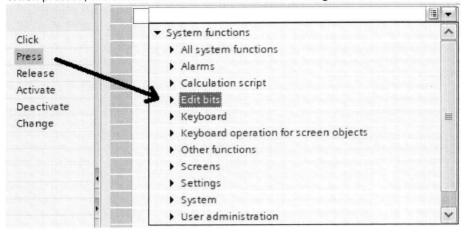

Press -> Edit bits -> Set bit

This will bring up the field, shown in pink, waiting to be connected to the variable defined in the global CPU Data Block.

If there were more CPUs we could enter any of these thanks to the great flexibility of the new Profinet protocol.

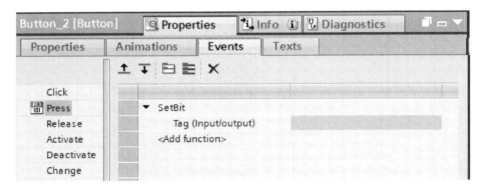

Click in the pink field, a key appears with three small dots.

By opening the path up to the global DB, the appropriate variable is selected here.

The TIA Portal editor helps us with a color code to understand if the variable we are going to connect is the correct one.

A blue label is shown if it is contained in the global DB (correct) or purple if it is in the local variables of the HMI, incorrect in our context.

There are other situations in which it will be right to connect to the HMI variables. The latter is HMI default tags table.

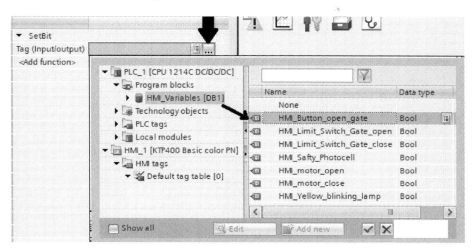

During this association, the global DB variable is automatically copied between the local HMI variables.

> The "HMI default tags table", in the HMI side, consent an additional setting for the refresh time.
> It should be 100 ms as it is similar to human reaction times.

When the button is released, the same bit must be reset.

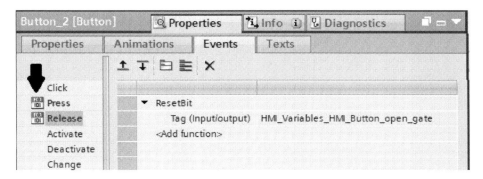

A purple labels in the left part of the print and required release commands that a script was created, in high level level language.
WinCC is designed to create these scripts and the programmer does not have to worry about them.
In case of rethink or error the whole script must be removed using the black cross.

Some objects do not require events, but only the association of the corresponding TAGs in the global data block.

Consider the pilot light, very useful for indicating the status of Boolean signals.

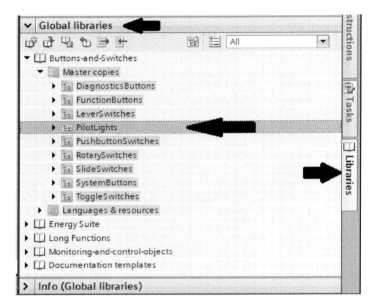

It is places in the WinCC global libraries, which are not very easy to find.

Follow the path shown in the image starting from the lower right corner of the WinCC window.

If there is no global library item click on the down arrows.
Set the TAg created in the Global Data Block to represent the status of the limit switches.

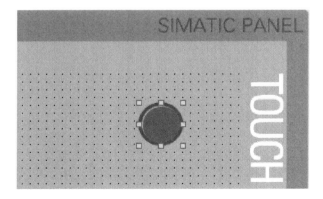

The next image shows where to act to select the TAG.

Remember that this is located in the global Data block located in the project tree in the leaf "Program blocks".

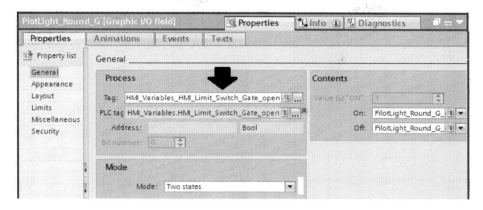

Suppose a pilot light represents the yellow blinking lamp, this should have update times that meet the requirements of the Shannon rule.

If the refresh times were equal to 1 second it could not follow the flashing at a frequency of 1Hz.

Refresh must be set to 100ms, in the HMI default tags table.

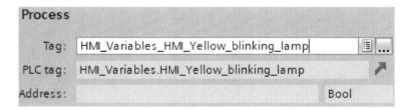

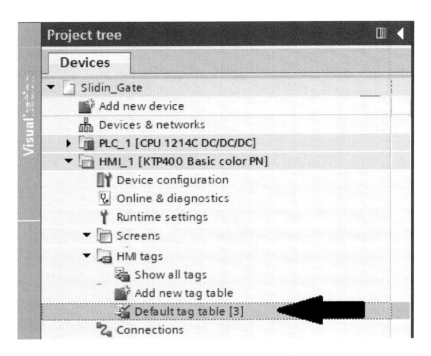

There are many fields in the HMI default tags table, it may be necessary to move the cursor to the right to make the "Acquisition Time" field visible, to be set at 100ms.

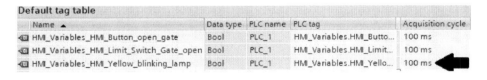

Name ▲	Data type	PLC name	PLC tag	Acquisition cycle
HMI_Variables_HMI_Button_open_gate	Bool	PLC_1	HMI_Variables.HMI_Butto...	100 ms
HMI_Variables_HMI_Limit_Switch_Gate_open	Bool	PLC_1	HMI_Variables.HMI_Limit...	100 ms
HMI_Variables_HMI_Yellow_blinking_lamp	Bool	PLC_1	HMI_Variables.HMI_Yello...	100 ms

In more complex programs it is necessary to categorize the variables by creating multiple tag tables with a name that remembers the function of the variables it contains.

Each type of standard data is allowed in the DBs, but for user-defined types they must first be defined in the project tree in PLC Data Type, then an array is created whose elements are this new type of data.

Mockup by G-Tronic

In manufacturing and design, a mockup, or mock-up, is a scale or full-size model of a design or device, used for teaching, demonstration, design evaluation, promotion, and other purposes.

A mockup is a prototype if it provides at least part of the functionality of a system and enables testing of a design and software program.

In manufacturing and design, a mockup, or mock-up, is a scale or full-size model of a design or device, used for teaching, demonstration, design evaluation, promotion, and other purposes.

A mockup is a prototype if it provides at least part of the functionality of a system and enables testing of a design and software program.

The G-Tronic Mock-ups are used by teachers mainly to shown step7 command to a students and simulate anomaly in mechanic parts.

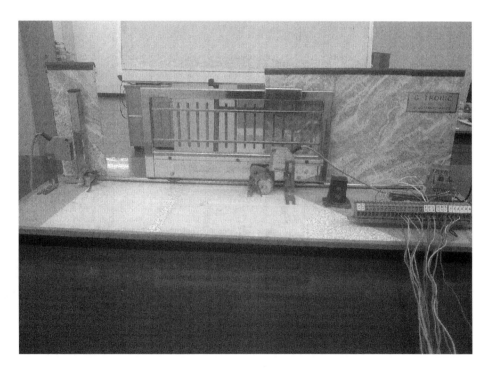

The first scale model produced by G-Tronic was the automatic gate. Many videos and tutorials have been published. In all textbooks used in vocational training courses in Italy is present. The basic educational value is high even if a PLC will not be installed in this type of real automation.

Marco Gottardo, has used this exercise since the early 1990s.

The educational value counts of:

- Photocell installation
- Installation of limit switches, idea of open contact and closed contact in an Automatic cycle.
- Reversal of DC motors
- Safety devices, flashing warning light.
- Basic connection to the PLC digital inputs and outputs.
- Connection to HMI interface, process variable exchange management

in the G-Tronic mockup real photocells are installed in order to train students in the management of objects that they will then find in the workplace.

The photocell installed on the mockup is the model FTQ-CBE, it is a reflection with reflector – polarized Light.

These photocells use antireflex device so only a coupled reflector can answear to the emitted light.

System si bases its functioning of a polarized band of light, and secure readings even when the object to be sensed has a very shiny surface.

The technical data afected by random reflections.

There are four main types of photocells.

The four types of photocells.

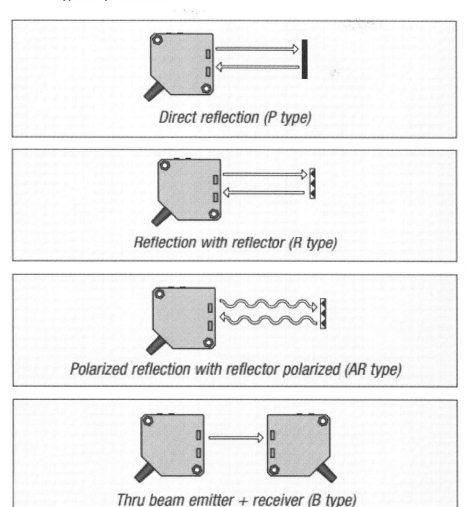

Direct reflection (P type)

Reflection with reflector (R type)

Polarized reflection with reflector polarized (AR type)

Thru beam emitter + receiver (B type)

Direct reflection (P type)

In this function type the emitter of the infrared light and the receiver are close and housed together.
The sensing is obtained by the reflection of the rays from the object.
Using these photocells it is important to bear in mind colour and type of surface of the object.
With opaque surfaces the sensing distance is affected by the colour of the object, light colours correspond to the maximum distances and vice versa.
In the case of shiny objects the effect of the surface is more important than the colour.

The sensing distance in the technical data is related to matt white paper.

Reflection with reflector (R type)
This photocell has emitter and receiver housing together.
The reflection of the light emitted is obtained by using one or more reflectors and the object sensing occurs when these rays are interrupted.
These photocells allow longer sensing distances as the rays emitted are almost totally reflected towards the receiver.

Reflection with reflector - polarized light (AR type)
Similar to the R type, these photocells use an antireflex device, the use of such a device, which bases its functioning on a polarized band of light, offers considerable advantages and secure readings even when the object to be ensed has a very shiny surface. They are not in the technical data afected by random reflections.

Thru beam emitter-receiver (B type)
These is the type in the mockup.
 In this type of function the emitter and receiver of infra-red light face each other.
Sensing is achieved when this barrier of light is interrupted, they have a high reception as there is no dispersion between emitter and receiver.
These photocells are therefore used for large distances where a high security of functioning is required.
M18 types are supplyable with shutter of various diameters to be screwed on to optic part of both photoelectric sensors.
This accessory permits detection of small objects in precision detecting applications.

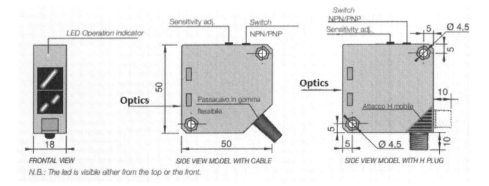

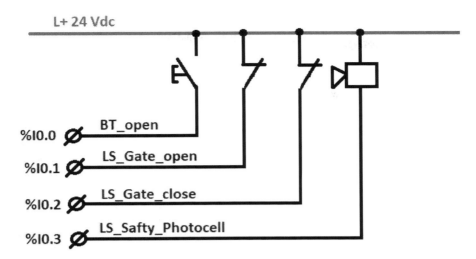

L+ 24 Vdc

%I0.0 ⌀   BT_open

%I0.1 ⌀   LS_Gate_open

%I0.2 ⌀   LS_Gate_close

%I0.3 ⌀   LS_Safty_Photocell

The digital inputs of the PLC are connected as shown in the schematic.

All the signals are internally referred to the same mass provided that there is a wire between M of the inputs and M of the internal power supply of the PLC. Signals must be bridged.

The sensors are all connected to the 24DC voltage line. The buttons are connected N.O. while the limit switches and the safety photocell are N.C.

In case of breakage or loss of one of the sensors, limit switch or photocell, the PLC receives the same signal of a possible intervention.

The gottardo's rule: When a contact is delegated to release a self-latching, it is acquired in the software as opposed to how it is inserted in the functional scheme.

The output signals from the PLC are of two types depending on the chosen CPU.
Relay outputs or transistor outputs.

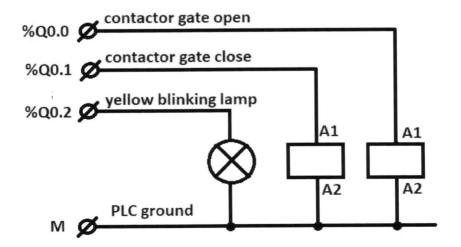

%Q0.0 ⌀   **contactor gate open**

%Q0.1 ⌀   **contactor gate close**

%Q0.2 ⌀   **yellow blinking lamp**

A1   A1

A2   A2

M ⌀   **PLC ground**

When the relay outputs are used, there are some limitations in the switching frequency, which hardly exceeds 2Hz in order not to damage them due to prolonged activation.

These are clean mechanical contacts that on the one hand show the% Qx.x physical outputs to which to connect the external actuators, internally they are instead connected to a common reference that we should set to the high level 24Vdc.

Obviously they are auxiliary relays and not contactor so we should not directly connect machine motors.

The outputs are designed to drive the coils of small power contactors.

To perform the reversing of a DC motor it is necessary to create an H bridge, like the one suggested in the diagram, using external relays.

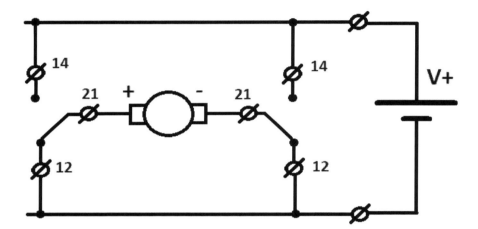

To the motor left there is the contacts of the KM1 relay, while on the right we have the contacts of the KM2.

The upper horizontal line is placed at the generator positive while the lower one is the ground.

Normally both the motor terminals are grounded so that they present a braking situation as required by the Lentz law.

Switching one of the two switches causes the current to flow in that direction in the motor, defining the direction of rotation.

It is left to the reader, with the use of a pencil, to trace the current in the meshes that develop and relate on the direction of rotation.

When both contacts are activated, both motor terminals are equipotential to the positive value, in the absence of a d.d.p. no electric current flows and therefore the motor does not transform energy into kinetics.

This H bridge is self-protected by short circuits to ground.

Numbers shown in the wiring diagram are the same as those visible in the socket of the real relay.

This helps us greatly during wiring.

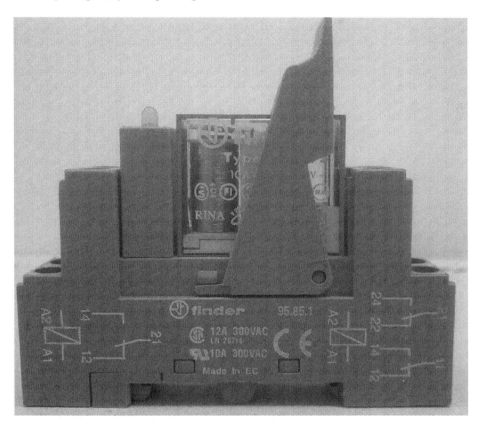

Note that the socket shows two possibilities, one on the left and one on the right.

The correct one depends on the relay we mount, in fact there are two-way or one-way models.

These relays produced by Finder have a signaling LED and often house the free recirculation diode.

The image shows the assembly of the two relays used for the construction of the bridge H.
These are housed in a standard Omega DIN rail.

The many necessary cables flow into a clear terminal block.

Note that the first group on the right is a 6-way bridge all grounded.

Sul lato sinistro dell'immagine vediamo il pulsante di apertura del cancello i cui collegamenti elettrici sono nascosti nella parte inferiore del mockup

A hole was made in the wooden plane the wires of this and other sensors slide along the special plastic concealed.

On the right side we can see the electromechanical limit switch, which supplies the signal when the gate is open.

The terminal N.O. it is not connected because the PLC just needs to interpret the N.C. connection, any logic inversion is software implemented.

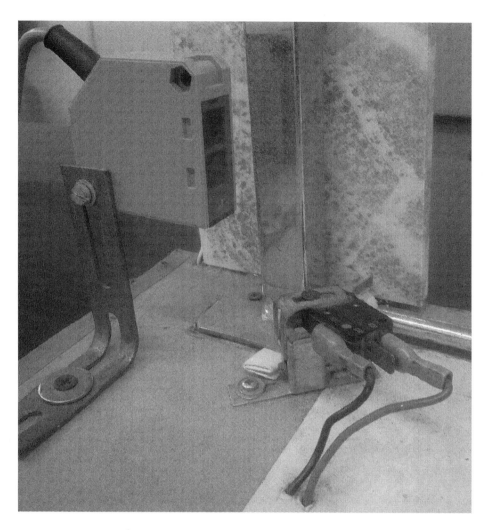

In this image we see the gate on the side of the closure where the closed side limit switch is installed.

Two of the three terminals are connected, the common wire and the N.C side, the red terminal is connect to +24DC referred to PLC ground.

On the same side is visible the receiver of the pair of devices forming the photocell.

In the next pictures of the students of the G-Tronic industrial automation school engaged in the assembly of the PLC and the HMI panel.

Students from all over the world are welcome, take your training period by email ad.noctis@gmail.com.
Accomodation is take in charge by G-Tronic.

Sliding gate program.

The semi-automatic gate with sliding door, moved by mechanical coupling to pinion and rack, is a mile stone in all automation training courses.
In this case, the beginner programmer will be able to choose the correct type of timer, to create a controlled square-wave oscillation, and the project the correct driver type for interfacing to the DC actuator.
Programmer need to know and apply the actual regulations for the installation and maintenance of these plants.
Like any automation problem, it is faced by carrying out the "interview phase" which consists of asking the customer about how the system should behave.
The question, in this case, is particularly simple because we speak of a normal domotic gate.

Warning: 3 seconds before every gear movement warn the users by a blinking yellow light at the frequency of a Hertz.
It is forbidden to remove any mechanical or electro mechanical safety guards.

Interview phase for the realization of the semi-automatic gate.

A sliding gate must be designed whose kinematic chain is composed of a pinion and rack coupling. The D.C. motor, supply at 24 volts, it is equipped with gears reduction in order to deliver the correctly torque to move the leaf.
The gate opening command consists of pressing a button, wired in normally open mode (N.O.), to which it is connected in parallel a normally open contact operated by a coded remote control.
Pressing the button activates an intermittent yellow blinking light at the frequency of one Hertz, but no movement occurs.
the people present near the gate will be warned that mechanical organs will be put into motion.
After three seconds, then at the third blink, the gate opens.
The blinking, associated with the movement, remains until the limit switch, of the complete opening, is stroke.
The mobile leaf will stay in the maximum opening position for 17 seconds, before restarting the blinking yellow signal.
A further 3 seconds will pass the motor for closing the gate.
The blinking yellow signal is active during movement and three seconds before this happens.
During the closing stroke the safety photocell could act with the effect of blocking the closing movement instantaneously.
In these position the sliding door will wait 3 seconds to allow the mechanical inertias to extinguish.
For greater moving masses a greater times will be necessary but three seconds are sufficient for practically all cases.

The internal reduction, to the gearmotor, requires these delay because of the high torques that develop in the kinematic chain constituted by the set of gears that constitute the reduction itself.

For example if the internal axis of the motor rotates at 1000, or more, R.P.M. while the reduction of the gear motor brings the foreign axis to 60 R.P.M. (or slightly more), a small residual movement of the outer axis is a non-trascurable velocity of the inner axis.

This speed could result in a high internal torque that corresponds to a high stress in the gear teeth.

A probable rupture will occur in the reversal event if this happens before everything is stopped.

With everything stopped we mean not only the external in movement masses but above all each internal gear of the kinematic chain.

In this case there is also an extra voltage problem on the active elements of the H bridge (power mosfet or BJT) because the motor, which is not stopped and not powered, behaves as a generator.

When a command at H bridge imposes the motion direction reversal, the Lenz voltage, of inverted polarity, is added to that supplied to the motor.

When the safety photocell intervenes, the closing motion is stopped, then expiration of the inertia is awaited, finally the gear is reversed and bringing the gate back to its maximum opening.

Next step is the resumes of normal cycle, so 17 seconds is waiting for to reignite the flashing light and 20 to restart the closing movement.

Obviously, if the obstacle is not remove and still engage the safety photocell line, the sliding gate will be at its maximum opening and remains for all the time the protection line is interrupted.

when the photocell is released, the normal cycle restarts, so the two timers of 17 and 20 seconds is driven and inserting a delay before the inversion.

When the sliding gate reaches the closed end, it has returned to the "zero machine" condition, therefore, as known from the definition of semi-automatic cycle, the machine waits for the consent of the operator before executing a new cycle.

What is a DB?

In Step 7 language, a DB or Data Block, is a well defined memory area where store a variables during the program elaboration.
There are two kind of DB.
1. Global DB,
2. Instance DB.

The Global DB contain a variables readable and writable from everywhere in the program ad by any kind of program block.
They are the default information interchange area between HMI and PLC.
The variables shown in the HMI panels are the user interface with the control unit.
In S7-300 versions it was customary to prevent the simultaneous opening of multiple global DBs.
The rule derived from the STL language structure also called AWL.
The blocks were opened with a special command:

      AUF DB1   //open global DB number 1, "OPN DB"

Opening a DB with this command automatically closes all the others previously opened.
This means that a load command does not create ambiguity on the variable to be loaded.
For example:

      L DBW 2   //Load the second word from the open DB

Destination of the Load command was ACCU 1 by default.
Direct uploading opens and points a variable using a single line of code.
For example

      L DB1.DBW 2   //load the same variable of previous example.

An instance DB is instead bound to a functional block, called in Step 7 "FB" or also "function with memory".
It is allocated automatically when the FB is called.
Contains the variables that the programmer has entered in the interface section of the FB.
In first approximation these variables represent the input and output pins of the function block we have created.
When the interface of an FB is changed, there is no longer any use of the old instance DB and therefore the block call appears red surrounded.
Inconsistence between instance DB and FB can be solved only deleting boot, FB instance and DB, and make a new call of the new FB block in the network.

Automatic sliding gate mechanical scheme.

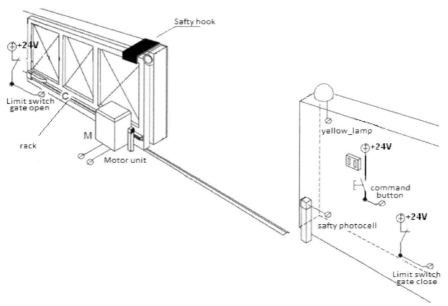

In the previous image the mechanical scheme of the semi-automatic sliding gate is shown.
In the next one, there is a mock up, useful in didactic laboratory, school, etc.

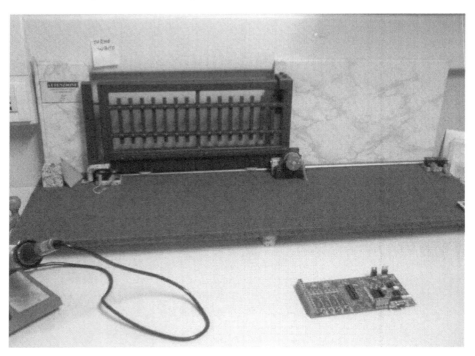

The mechanical scheme, when more complex than this example, is called flussogram or tube and instrument diagram, also known as **P&I** or even P&Id.

The second document, which is also of fundamental importance, is the functional scheme.

The functional scheme represents the algorithm implemented in the software and not the real electromechanical devices.

According to this principle, a direct correspondence with the real sequence constructed with electromechanical relays and contactors should not be sought.

For example:

> **The Gottardo's Roule,** each limit switch's contact, wired normally close, which is delegated to release the self-retainer, (self retain or self-latching rung) will appear in the software inverted respect to the schematic. In almost all the case it will appear normally open on the software.

When the self-retaining segment is made using contacts displayed on the HMI, no state reversal occurs. The rule is not contradictory as it considers physical switch contacts.

The fundamental elements of functional logic are:
1. Power Line, horizontal at the top, indicated with L + or L if powered in DC or AC. Not being an electric circuit but an algorithm to be implemented in the internal logic of the PLC through the software is more sensible to be always continuous.
2. Return line, indicated with M (mass as closing of a line L +) or N (neutral as closing of an alternating current line).
3. Derivations, which lower the logical flow downwards. In the true functional, each segment starts from a descent and does not derive horizontally from the previous segment. Therefore, in the example that follows the thermal is not a hardware redundancy since its state is only a bit internal to the logic of the PLC.
4. Contact in closing, or N.O. (ie normally open wired), with a clean contact appearance designed to the left of the vertical descent line.
5. Contact in opening or N.C. (ie normally closed wired), with a clean contact appearance designed to the right of the vertical descent line.
6. Timed coil delayed on excitation and its opening and closing contact.
7. Timed coil delayed after de-excitation (released delayed) and its contact in opening and closing.
8. Counter, represented as a rectangular load coil but with up, down, set and reset inputs. The preset value must also be represented.

The useful symbols for writing a functional are summarized in the image below. As we can see, the triangles on the limit switchs like the closing bars are not essential since the various contacts represent only the internal Boolean bit status or present on the terminal board.

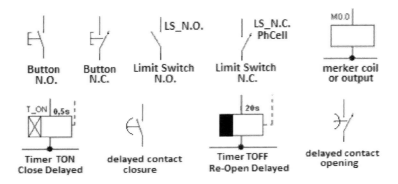

| Button N.O. | Button N.C. | Limit Switch N.O. | Limit Switch N.C. | merker coil or output |

| Timer TON Close Delayed | delayed contact closure | Timer TOFF Re-Open Delayed | delayed contact opening |

In the following picture the functional diagram of the sliding semi-automatic gate.

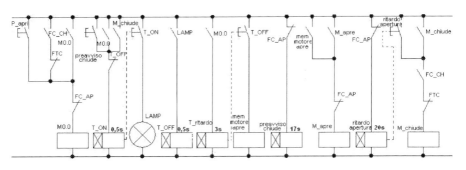

Obviously this is one of the solutions, but not the only one.

In the following pages, segments having the same overall function will be analyzed, even if they have small differences with respect to this scheme.

44

Network 1

The purpose of the first segment is to activate a boolean memory, on the merker area, when the open function button is pressed or in parallel the radio command from the remote control arrives (contact not shown).

The SET of this marker does not involve direct action on the motor.

These boolean memory remains self-holding (or self retain or same time self-latching) until the sliding gate reaches the maximum opening so it strike the "limit switch gate open" connect to the digital input %I0.1.

This memory can also be activated if, during the closing stroke, the photocell is interrupted.

The interruption of the photocell line when the gate is in the closed position, on the side detected by "limit_switch_gate_close", connect at the digital input %I0.3, has no effect.

Network 2

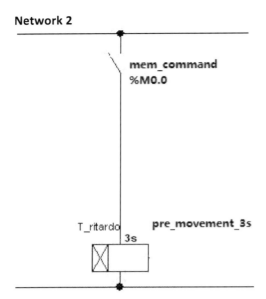

The command Button placed in a self retain memory, drive a timer that insert a three seconds delay before act the opening.

The activated timer is of the TON type.

As foreseen by the directive iEC61131C -3, it introduces a delay to the controlled output equal to the value set in milliseconds.

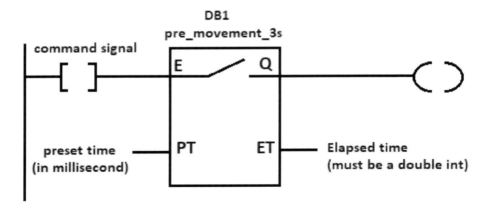

The one shown is a timer with delayed closing action. The IEC name is "TON".
It acts on a boolean within its instance DB at the address indicated by ".Q"
To setup the PT signal (preset time) write the value in millisecond, in example 3000.
The ET (Elapsed Time) signal is a double int that need a 32bits allocation in memory, always in a DB.

Network 3

IEC timers, as we will see better, are functions with memory, which support the results on an instance data block.

This segment uses the output contact of a timer placed in the data block DB1.DBX6.0

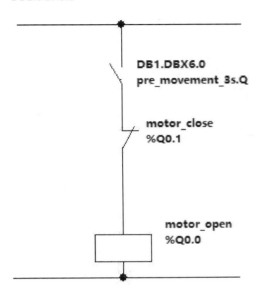

When the boolean output contact of the timer closes the motor starts.

For security reasons, this is delayed by at least three seconds after the operator's command. in the meantime the yellow flashing signal warns users near the machine of the imminent danger situation.

Network 4

This network implements the oscillator semi-period of for the yellow lamp.
During this half period the lamp is on.
A combinatorial logic net defines the temporal instant in which the flashing lamp is active.

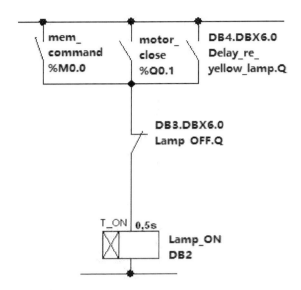

From the left the contact of the manual opening command internal memory, the closing motor signal, the open waiting timeout.

TON timer, generate on-delay instruction to delay setting of the Q output by the programmed time PT, sometimes called **Preset Time**.

The instruction is started when the result of logic operation (RLO), also called RLC, at input IN changes from "0" to "1" (positive signal edge).

The programmed time PT begins when the instruction starts.
When the time PT has elapsed, the output Q has the signal state "1".
Output Q remains set as long as the start input is still "1".

When the signal state at the start input changes from "1" to "0", the Q output is reset.

The timer function is started again when a new positive signal edge is detected at the start input so the time ramp outputted in a 32 bit location by ET output pin is restarted.
The timer name is actually assigned to the instance data block that is automatically generated when the timer is recalled.

The current time value can be queried at the ET output. The timer value starts at T#0s and ends when the value of the time duration PT is reached.

The ET output is reset as soon as the signal state at the IN input changes to "0".

Each call of the "Generate on-delay" instruction must be assigned to an IEC timer in which the instruction data is stored.

Be careful never to duplicate the timers with copy and paste. They will not work.

This network implement a blinking warning that alert users about gears is going into movement.

Visual signal consist in **1Hz** flashing yellow lamp, driven by two TON timers.

Only the first TON timer can drive the lamp because the second one generate only a trigger signal and not a latch, like is possible deduce analyzing the run-time diagram.

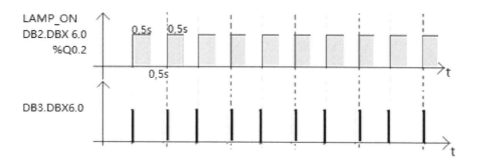

The frequency definition is deduced from the inverse of the period. The unit of measurement is the inverse of the time that is called Hertz.

$$f = \frac{1}{T}$$

$$Hz = \frac{1}{s} = s^{-1}$$

Network 5

The second timer TON generates the reset trigger for the first, causing the output to oscillate.

During this time when the flashing light is off T_OFF.

However this time is not the complementary of the previous one, so we do not obtain a complementary flashing by connecting a second lamp to this timer.

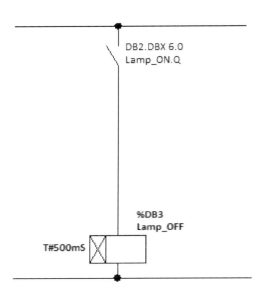

As in the case of the previous timer, the instance data block is renamed.
As already noted, the instance data block is automatically generated and it is possible at this time to assign the new name.

However, in case of forgetfulness it is possible to rename the data block to the rear by making an appropriate right-click sequence.

In this segment the complementary ON action of the yellow lamp is not present but only the trigger signal, lasting about one millisecond.
For clarity, analyze the time diagram of the previous page.

These segment do not generate a half period latch.

Network 6

After the opening stroke, the moving part meets the maximum opening limit switch.

This is wired normally closed, so the action performs the switching "normal 1-> pressed 0".

These mean the signal fall down from 24Vdc present to 0 on the PLC's I/O.

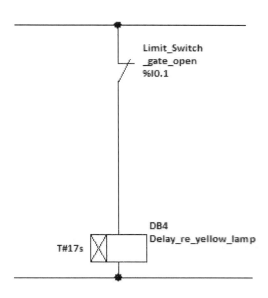

The zero state on the PLC input activates a delay timer 17th seconds long.

If the 17 second timer is passed its contact turn to present, (signal rise 0 to logic 1), and the yellow flashing lamp is driven.

It is useful to warns the users of the imminent reclosing maneuver, or the opening command key has been switched, or the gate is in closing maneuver (motor is ON).

This segment does not drive the motor at least three seconds of warning are required by the flashing yellow lamp.

It is job of another timer to start the engine to close it.
This will be preset 3 seconds longer and is implemented in the next segment.

Network 7

The same signal that drives the previous segment controls a 20-second timer.
This act the gate motor to open it.

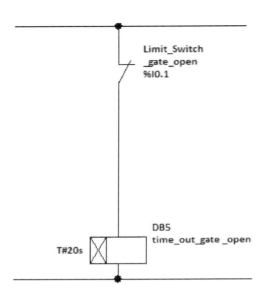

The normally closed contact of this timer will be used to support self-latching (self retain) in subsequent segments.

To use these signal is necessary to access, with property sequence of clik, to the istance data block.

An example of access to the boolean output signal is shown below.

Time_out_gate_open.Q

Network 8

The segment is an self-latching command to start the motor to the close side.
The run to close state is released when the limit switch is reach or safety photocell is engage.

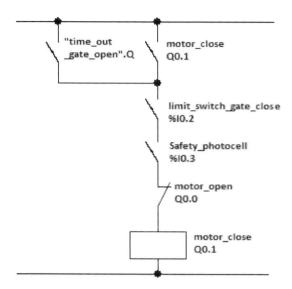

The normally closed switch, which precedes the coil, is the interlock.
It has the same function as the one inserted in segment number 3.

This technique is designed to introduce software protection from possible incorrect commands, for example the simultaneous request for forward and reverse run of the motor.
It is important to know that software protection guarantees up to the PLC terminals, but there could be an electromechanical anomaly.

Thermal stress can lead to the fusion of the electromechanical contacts of the contactors.

Due to the electric arcs, the fusion of the contacts can be carried out in the same way as the electrode welding takes place.

In the case of DC circuits it is possible to limit the arcs by introducing the anti-parallel diode of recirculation to the contacts.

to ensure that the contacts of the remote switch are not soldered it is necessary to introduce feedback from the field. Assemble auxiliary contacts on the contactor that switch mechanically together with the power lines.
It is therefore easy to manage any anomaly via software.

The implementation of the functional scheme makes the software implementation independent of the CPU model to be used.

TIA Portal V15_1 also allows configuration of obsolete models such as the S7-300 and S7-400 series.

As an example we see how the automatic gate program can be upload into an old S7-313C CPU.

This CPU will be connected to the programmer via the MPI serial protocol, now in disuse but widely present in industrial plants.

The question is, is it possible to configure the USB to MPI adapter using TIA Portal V15_1 drivers?

Yes it is. The test was also carried out with the latest version of the Win10 operating system.

In the following pages we will see how it is possible to use the same program in the various generations and CPU models.

Create a TIA 15_1 project with S7-300 CPU.

Start by double clicking on the TIA Portal V15_1 icon on the desk top.
If the user licenses are well installed then, after opening the hardware catalog the CPUs are visible and can be removed.
If a red cockade appears above the CPU icons it means that the Licens administrator tool does not work well or there are no valid licenses.

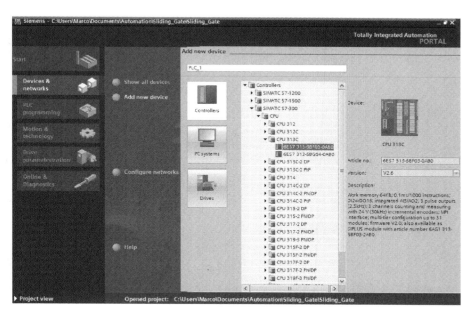

In some cases it is necessary, in windows 10, to act on the operating properties of the DLL of the licens manager tool.
Right click on the link on the desktop. Open the file Path.

Programmi › Siemens › Automation › Automation License Manager › almapp

Nome ᐱ	Ultima modifica	Tipo	Dimensione
almapp64x.exe	02/02/2017 14:14	Applicazione	3.006 KB
almaxc64x.dll	02/02/2017 14:12	Estensione dell'ap...	341 KB
AlmReporting.exe	02/02/2017 14:12	Applicazione	920 KB
AlmReportingCfg.exe	02/02/2017 14:11	Applicazione	872 KB

On each icon, right click, change compatibility for Win7, for all users. Also set the execution as an administrator.

It is good to apply this trick also for the main launch file in the appropriate folder.
Probably Siemens will solve these compatibility problems in the next versions.

The old S7-300 systems resemble the new 1500 because they are mounted on an aluminum guide called a rack.

As we can see, to the right of the CPU there are numbered slots of which position 3 is not available.

This position is reserved for a particular communication block, the IM card.

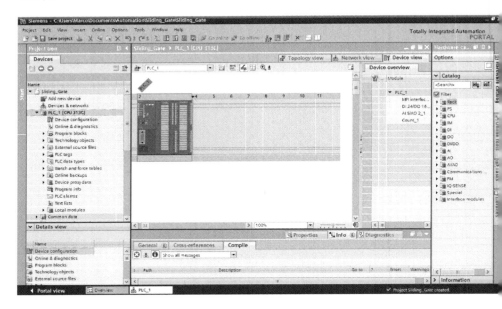

From the catalog, visible on the right panel, it is possible to take the I/O expansion blocks to be inserted in the free slots.

It is good practice to first insert the analog expansions and in the rightmost slots the digital ones, in any case before the inputs and then the outputs.

This convention is also used in the current versions of the S7-1200 and S7-1500 PLCs.

The left panel represents the project tree.

In this section it is possible to see the interconnections between PLC stations and HMI operator panels, through one or more transmission protocols.

Different protocols, including Profibus (obsolete) and Profinet, will be able to coexist, through appropriate conversion hardware.

The network interconnections of the various components are visible in the network view window.

It is also possible to insert non-Siemens components in the network as long as the manufacturer supplies the GSDs (general station description files) that act as drivers on TIA Portal.

In the Option menus the command "manage the general description files", after downloading them from the manufacturer's website.

Regardless of the protocol chosen, in this image, MPI, right click on the colored square that represents the communication port.
The colors have been standardized to green for Profinet, Viola for Profibus, orange for MPI.
There are other protocols but less used in this context.

Once the station is inserted it is good to change the name on the project tree so that it takes on a concrete meaning in the context of the whole program.

It should be remembered that the TIA Portal platform was created for large and distributed systems in which a large number of PLCs with relevant inverters and HMIs are interconnected.

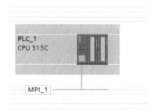

After the subnet is inserted, the infrastructure must be designed and then IP addresses assigned, when Profinet, or the node number in case of Profibus or MPI.

A connection test is necessary to test the correct installation of the drivers.

An orange theme in some parts of the page indicates that the connection is established.

TIA Portal can connect simultaneously with multiple plant sections.
In the image we see how the system asks with which device you want to go to online.

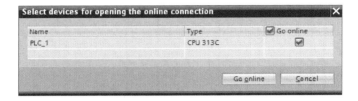

If the MPI interface is correctly installed, you will get to the following screen which will scan the accessible nodes and detect if the station is correctly configured.

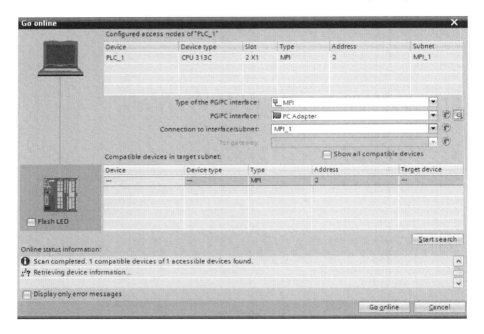

The scan shown has detected only one station online.
In case there were more PLCs interconnected they are shown in list form.
In order to easily recognize each PLC, it is necessary to combine a meaningful name with the CPU with respect to the industrial system, for example Conveyor control, hopper control, grinder control, etc.
The MPI protocol, mentioned here, derives from the RS485 serial line, similarly to the Profibus, but is limited in number of nodes.
The transmission speed of the Profibus reaches up to 12Mb and thanks to the use of repeaters can reach up to 128 units.

TIA Portal V15 project with S71511C CPU.

Today the most powerful CPUs of Siemens are the 1500 series that replace the previous S7-400 series, now obsolete.

These CPUs are mounted on a dedicated aluminum rail and not in Omega DIN as the 1200.

These models have a display on which the system statuses are shown.
Some interventions are also allowed.

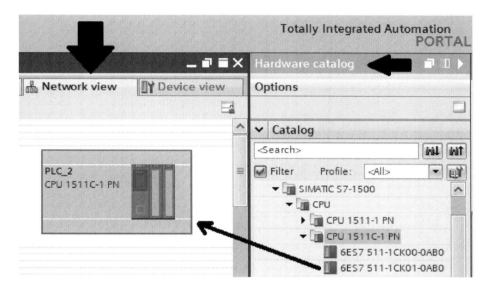

The main CPU 1511C-1 PN features are.

The CPU have a display above, with large work memory 175 KB code and 1 MB data.
The cycle time is very quick and permit a 60 ns bit instruction time.

There is a 4-stage protection concept, technology functions:
- motion control,
- closed-loop control,
- counting & measuring;
- tracing;

The integrated PROFINET IO controller, supports RT/IRT, performance upgrade PROFINET V2.3, 2 ports, I-device, MRP, MRPD, transport protocol TCP/IP, secure Open User Communication, S7 communication, **Web server**, DNS client, OPC UA server data access, constant bus cycle time, routing; Runtime options.
The firmware in the later 2019 was V2.5 version.

The I/O profile is wide with DI16/DQ16, AI5/AQ2.

The unit can be expanded with 16DIxDC24V digital input module, grouping 16, 16DQxDC24V/0,5A digital output module, grouping 16,

The analog features are
4xU/I AI analog input module, AI 1xRTD, 16-bit, grouping in 5;
2xU/I AQ analog output module, 16-bit, grouping 2;

The High speed features are
6 channels for counting and measuring with incremental encoders 24 V (up to 100 kHz); 4 channels for PTO, pulse-width modulation, frequency output (up to 100 kHz).

If it were not so expensive it would be the best choice to equip educational workshops.

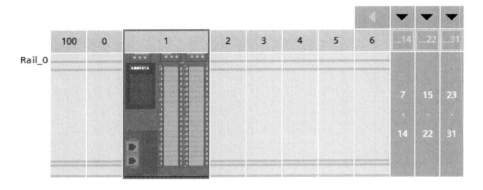

The rail is a dedicated aluminum profile and cannot be replaced with different elements.

The Omega standard rail is not useful for replacement.

The connectors have a less robust and manageable appearance than those of the previous S7-300 and S7-400 series.

The zero slot is designed to house a power supply suitable for energizing the system.
According to industrial standards this must be taken from a single phase power line at 24V DC.

A standard power supply, which does not provide special possibilities to divide the load towards normal I/O is at least 25W, in example the model

6ES7 505-0KA00-0AB0 that supplies the operating voltage for the S7-1500 backplane bus.

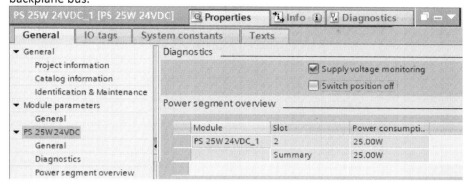

The assembly of the PLC components takes place with the aid of a backplane for the connection of the buses to the next module.

The power supplies also provide diagnostics to the central processor as shown in the figure.

The Power Modules supply more energy to the system but are also able to distribute it better to the various modules through a system called Front wall Wiring.

Load current supply 190 W, 120/230 VAC model 6EP1333-4BA00

The old compact CPUs of the S7-300 series numbered the expansions starting from the bottom of the bus. This is no longer true for the new S7-1500 series.

To discovery the connection points of the machine board to the CPU it is necessary to query the properties.

The addresses of the digital inputs and outputs are shown, useful in the example of the automatic gate, in addition the analogs, the high-speed counters and all the other I/O.

Looking at the table, we note that the first available digital input is at address% I10.0, so the tags table must be filled in taking into account the offset compare of the same solution for CPU 1214C.

There is the possibility of automatically changing the addresses remapping them in the Tags table.

Module	Rack	Slot	I address	Q address	Type	Article no.	Firmware
	0	100					
Power supply slot	0	0					
▼ PLC_2	0	1			CPU 1511C-1 PN	6ES7 511-1CK01-0AB0	V2.5
AI 5/AQ 2_1	0	1 8	0..9	0..3	AI 5/AQ 2		
DI 16/DQ 16_1	0	1 9	10..11	4..5	DI 16/DQ 16		
HSC_1	0	1 16	12..27	6..17	HSC		
HSC_2	0	1 17	28..43	18..29	HSC		
HSC_3	0	1 18	44..59	30..41	HSC		
HSC_4	0	1 19	60..75	42..53	HSC		
HSC_5	0	1 20	76..91	54..65	HSC		
HSC_6	0	1 21	92..107	66..77	HSC		
Pulse_1	0	1 32	108..111	78..89	PWM		
Pulse_2	0	1 33	112..115	90..101	PWM		
Pulse_3	0	1 34	116..119	102..113	PWM		
Pulse_4	0	1 35	120..123	114..125	PWM		
▶ PROFINET interface_1	0	1 X1			PROFINET interface		

The default tag table shown below contains the correct labels and address for the example of which is the main theme of this book.

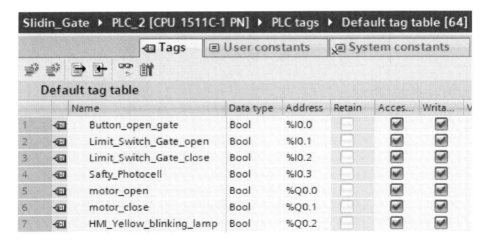

Slidin_Gate ▶ PLC_2 [CPU 1511C-1 PN] ▶ PLC tags ▶ Default tag table [64]

	🔲 Tags	🔲 User constants	🔲 System constants

Default tag table

		Name	Data type	Address	Retain	Acces...	Writa...	V
1	🔷	Button_open_gate	Bool	%I0.0	☐	☑	☑	
2	🔷	Limit_Switch_Gate_open	Bool	%I0.1	☐	☑	☑	
3	🔷	Limit_Switch_Gate_close	Bool	%I0.2	☐	☑	☑	
4	🔷	Safty_Photocell	Bool	%I0.3	☐	☑	☑	
5	🔷	motor_open	Bool	%Q0.0	☐	☑	☑	
6	🔷	motor_close	Bool	%Q0.1	☐	☑	☑	
7	🔷	HMI_Yellow_blinking_lamp	Bool	%Q0.2	☐	☑	☑	

The limit switches such as the photocell will be wired N.C. while the command button N.O.

An entire chapter will be devoted to wiring and wiring diagrams.

CPU 1511C-1 PN

The compact CPUs of the FAMILY 1500 "C" are the most suitable for equipping the educational laboratory because they offer features of completeness and power that are convenient compared to the cost.

However, this is still a bit high but bearing in mind that the instrument that is acquired is highly professional and valid also for medium-sized plants, it is still convenient compared to the purchase of separate components.

There is also a starter Kit that includes a power supply, the compact CPU, and an aluminum rack guide in addition to the Basic version of Step7 and TIA Portal V15.
All CPUs in the SIMATIC S7-1500 product family have a display with extensive text information.

The display shows information on the order numbers, the firmware version and the serial numbers of all connected modules; it is also possible to set the IP address of the CPU and make other network settings directly on site, without a programming device.

The display shows the error messages directly as signaling in extended text thus allowing the customer to reduce downtime.

The integrated system diagnostics is activated by default for the CPUs. The different types of diagnostics are configured instead of programmed.

System diagnostics information is displayed uniformly and in full text on the CPU display, in STEP 7, on the HMI and on the web server itself for drive messages.

This information is available both with the CPU in RUN and in STOP. If new hardware components are configured, the diagnostic information is updated automatically.

There are two compact CPU1500 versions with these technical features.

	CPU 1511C-1 PN	CPU 1512C-1 PN
Integrated analog input/output	5 input/2 output	5 input/2 output
Integrated digital input/output	16 inputi/16 output	32 input/32 output
High speed counters	6	6
Pulse genarotors • PWM (pulse width modulation) • PTO (Pulse Train Output or stepper motor control) • Frequency output	4 PTO or 4 PWM	4 PTO or 4 PWM

The CPU contains the IEC61131-3C operating system that runs the user program. The user program is located on the SIMATIC memory card and is processed in the working memory of the CPU.

Integrated technological functions

The CPUs of the SIMATIC S7-1500 family support the motion control functions. STEP 7 provides standardized blocks according to PLCopen for configuring and connecting a drive to the CPU.

Motion Control supports speed, positioning and synchronous axes (synchronization without setting the synchronization position) as well as external encoders, cams, cam tracks and measuring inputs.

high speed counters.

The counting functions (HSC) are equivalent to those of the TM Count 2x24 card.
It is possible to connect 24V encoders with channels A, B, N. The encoders that can be connected are:
Incremental encoders with N signal:

Signals A, B and N are connected through properly marked connections. Signals A and B are both encoder signals 90 ° out of phase. N is the zero mark signal that provides a pulse per revolution.

A maximum of 4 encoders (A, B, N) can be acquired on the CPU 1511C. In the CPU 1512C the limit remains 6.

Incremental encoders without N signal:
Signals A and B are connected through properly marked connections. Signals A and B are both signals
of the encoder 90 ° out of phase.

Pulse generators without direction signal: The counting signal is connected to connection A.

Pulse generators with direction signal: The counting signal is connected to connection A. The direction signal is connected to connection B.
Pulse generators with up / down counting signal: The up counting signal is connected to connection A.

The count down signal is connected to connection B.
The counting inputs are in common with the digital inputs.

Therefore by enabling a counter I will not have the corresponding digital inputs available.

Apply an encoder to the automatic gate

The use of an encoder for a domestic automatic gate oversize the problem. It is useful for educational completeness.
in this first volume of the didactic series only the encoder hardware is shown and the sofytware studies and the related axis control exercises are referred to a specific volume.
After reading the subsequent books in the series, the new technician is advised to try to trace the position of the sliding leaf and display it on the HMI.

Siemens incremental encoder

The sensor has seven connection wires towards the outside.
The first two are the usual D.C. which can vary from 5 up to 30V (check model by model on the databook).

Two are phase A and its denied, two for phase B and its denied, one for the zero bit, often indicated by Z. This is used to detect the complete revolution and thus save the current count value in a 'another Word to add to the current partial to reconstruct the whole thing

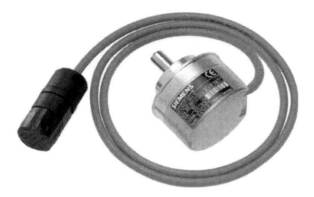

Schema di collegamento per encoder incrementale Siemens 6FX 2001-4 (Up = 24 V; HTL)

La figura seguente mostra lo schema di collegamento di un encoder incrementale Siemens 6FX 2001-4xxxx (Up = 24 V; HTL):

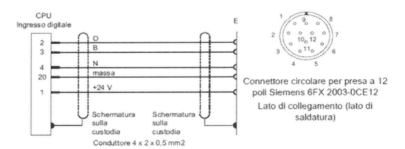

The encoder acquisition occurs through the use of HSCs or fast counters.

Compact CPUs may have terminals with multiple functions, such as digital input or high-speed counter.

If you want to use the standard inputs as fast counters, you need to disable the digital anti-bounce filters. on the properties of the CPU go to Digital Inputs.

TIA Portal V15 project with S71214C CPU.

The new CPUs of the S71200 or S71500 series have Profinet as their native protocol.

As for the predecessor, the Profibus, they were released by the PI consortium, a software house that deals with industrial real time applications.

Click on new project and provide the meaningful name. When we should develop a work for the company there will hardly be a clear name but a committed code, for example C19_2743.

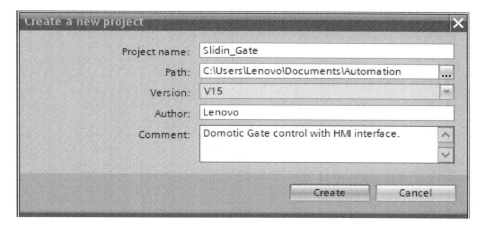

From the hardware catalog take the CPU model, and insert it in the network view. We take the HMI panel and interconnect via Profinet assigning the IP addresses.

Drag and drop the CPU from the right panel in the graphic area that represents the network system.
Drag the operator panel as well. For this example, the KTP400 basic Color PN model is sufficient.
This measures four inches and has the Profinet door.
The limitations it involves are not important for this example.

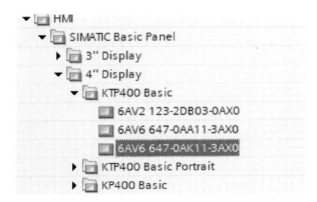

IP addresses can be set simply after viewing them by pressing the button that shows a small eye.

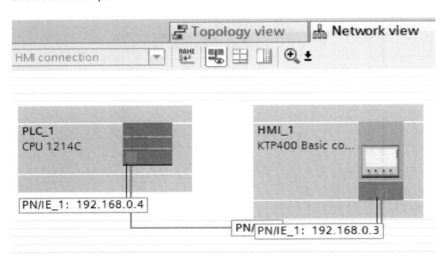

If the number of Profinet devices increases or you integrate into a pre-existing system, a network switch is need.
Do not use devices created for office or home use in industrial plants.
The hub switch called **Scalance** are produced by Siemens for mounting on industrial electrical panels.
For the moment it is sufficient to say that it needs an electrical certification for the intended use.

The main CPU 1214C DC/DC/DC features are.

The S71200 series has now reached the 3 firmware version indicated with the number **40** in the abbreviation 6ES7 214-1AG**40**-0XB0.

The old CPUs can be upgraded using an original Siemens SD card, only 24 Mbyte model, the updated firmware is available on the manufacturer's website.

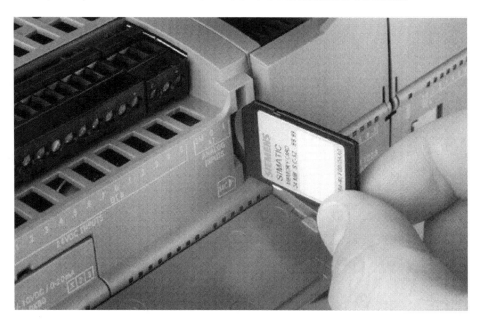

The SD cards, SMC calls (SIMATIC Memory Card) also allow to download the CPU without STEP 7 TIA Portal software or computer station.

If the program was created on a computer with the TIA Portal, it is also automatically copied to the Simatic Memory Card when downloaded via the Profinet port on the CPU.
We can now shift CPU to CPU by copying the program into multiple identical plant samples.
It is also possible to send the software with the email and copy it to the SMC to install it in the station without using the TIA Portal.
This applies to both the 1200 models and the 1500 models.
Only the firmware version 40 can work with the simulator and can be improved for example in some integrated functions such as PWm and PTO.

They are halfway between the S7-200 series and the S7-300 series.
From the first they derive as a natural evolution while from the second the programming style and the IEC 61131 mode, or the division into blocks, 32-bit timers, etc.

It has wide Work memory 100 KB; 24VDC power supply with DI14 x 24VDC SINK/SOURCE, DQ10 x 24VDC and AI2 on board.

it has 6 high-speed counters channels that allow the connection of as many encoders in single phase frequency mode or 3 encoders if in counter mode that each engage two digital inputs.

the pulse outputs allow to command with a PWM signal a possible MOSFET interface for the speed control of a DC motor. The same PWM can control a thermoresistance in order to modulate the heat transmitted to a certain quantity of liquid.
In this case the duty cycle can be integrated into a PID control loop for automatic adjustment.

signal board expands on-board I/O; up to 3 communication modules for serial communication; up to 8 signal modules for I/O expansion; 0.04 ms/1000 instructions; PROFINET interface for programming, HMI and PLC to PLC communication.

Data types table for CPU 1200

The PLC is a computer for industrial control use so, like all computers, it manipulates data with their numeric formats.

The following table shows the formats universally defined by the IEC61131-3C standard which regulates the PLCs.

Data Type	Dimensions (bit)	Field	Example of constant allocation
Bool	1	0 ... 1	TRUE, FALSE, O, 1
Byte	8	16#00 ... 16#FF	16#12, 16#AB
Word	16	16#0000 ... 16#FFFF	16#ABCD, 16#0001
DWord	32	16#00000000 ... 16#FFFFFFFF	16#02468ACE
Char	8	16#00 ... 16#FF	'A', 'r', '@'
Sint	8	-128 ... 127	123,-123
Int	16	-32.768 ... 32.767	123, -123
Dint	32	-2.147.483.648 ... 2.147.483.647	123, -123
USInt	8	0 ... 255	123
UInt	16	0 ... 65.535	123
UDInt	32	0 ... 4.294.967.295	123
Real	32	$+/-1{,}18 \times 10^{-38} ... +/-3{,}40 \times 10^{38}$	123,456, -3,4, -1,2E+12, 3,4E-3
LReal	64	$+/-2{,}23 \times 10^{-308} ... +/-1{,}79 \times 10^{308}$	12345.123456789 -1.2E+40
Time	32	T#-24d_20h_31 m_23s_648ms ... T#24d_20h_31 m_23s_647ms Salvato come: - 2,147.483,648 ms ... +2,147,483,647 ms	T#5m_30s 5#-2d T#1d_2h_15m_30x_45ms
String	Variable	0 ... 254 characters (size in bytes)	'ABC'

PLC 1200 moduli di comunicazione e espansione .

The S7-1200 series PLCs have performance comparable to those of the previous S7-300 series, and in some cases show improvements and greater flexibility.
In reality the 1200 series replaces the 200 of which it inherits the basic principles mixing them with that of the 300/400.

In the image we see an S7-1200 model 1214C, which integrates a good number of I / O in the central module.
A typical expansion is shown in which to the left of the CPU the communication modules are mounted and to the right the I / O expansions.

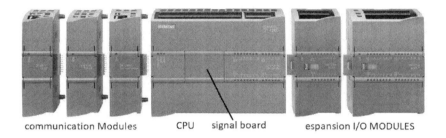

communication Modules   CPU   signal board   espansion I/O MODULES

There are communication modules for all communication protocols from serial to WiFi.

The RS485 and RS232 communication modules are suitable for point-to-point serial connections, based on characters.
The library works with the USS drive protocol and the Modbus RTU Master and Slave protocols are included in the SIMATIC STEP 7 Basic engineering system.
Regarding the Profibus master slave communication there are two new communication modules (CM) that facilitate the connection of S7-1200 to an existing PROFIBUS network.

Up to 16 field devices can be connected as DP slaves to the DP master CM 1243-5, for example the ET 200 decentralized peripheral unit. The S7-1200 can operate as a DP slave with the CM 1242-5 and can therefore be connected to any other DP master.

Both modules are easily connected to the left-side CPU backplane.
By adding the GPRS communication processor, the S7-1200 CPU supports simple Telecontrol applications for monitoring and controlling stations distributed via the GPRS (General Packet Radio Service) service.
The GPRS allows the sending by the CPU of SMS messages useful for diagnostics and remote intervention.

Clock flags on CPUs 1500 and 1200 for flashing light signaling.

As with the S7-300 and 400 CPUs, the CPUs of the 1500 and 1200 families also have flashing system bits that can be configured in the TIA Portal by accessing the CPU properties, right-clicking on the unit icon in the project tree. As shown in the images, the section is divided into two Bytes, of which we have the freedom to set the offset address.

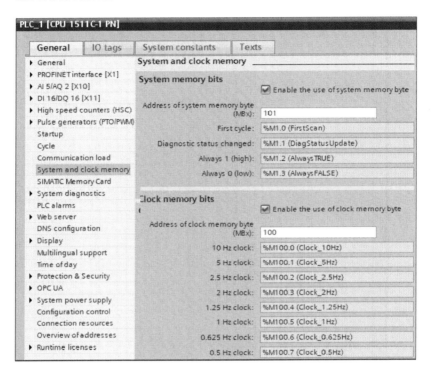

It is customary to set byte 100 to the flashing function.
Pay attention to the fact that by default you set byte 0 which could overlap with Boolean contacts that you previously used in your program causing serious problems.

In byte 101 the first 4 bits are assigned to very high system functions, for example a bit that is valid only at the first cycle of scans allowing the launch of an initialization routine, or a bit always low useful to perform non-segment bypassing. tested or obsolete in the context of the program.

Note that all the hardware settings are accessible from this screen, such as the management of the webserver (to activate the dataloggers and other), the OPC server (to make the DBs accessible from an industrial PC or SCADA system), alarm management , interrupts, system clock and much more.

Filling the tags table.

The first step common to any CPU hardware on which it will be implemented is the symbols table as know as Tags Table.

With the advent of TIA Portal the name becomes default Tags Table.

The Tags table shows all the addresses that have a physical terminal and the memories in the Merker area.

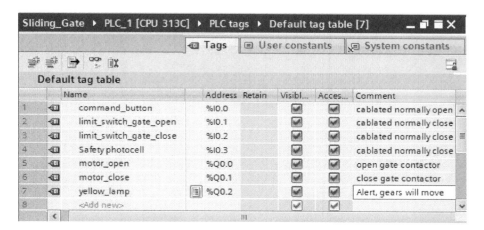

Note: In this table the Boolean markers, about the sliding gate, must be indicated. Looking at the first segment of the functional diagram, the address M0.0 mem_command appears.

This will be inserted with the addition of a comment, in example "pre opening command memory".

This table is <u>not</u> the right place to perform data exchange with HMI devices.

The internal variables, useful for turning on pilot lights or for listening to virtualized buttons in the HMI panel find natural placement in global Data Blocks.

> The variables that by their meaning in the context of the automatic cycle, after a control fault, a stop, a power failure, must keep the value prior to the event, will be defined as retentive type by click in the Retain column.

It is possible to indicate that the tag is directly accessible from the HMI panel by click in the accessible column.

Network 1: mem command pressed

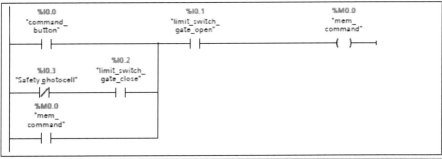

Symbol	Address	Type	Comment
"command_button"	%I0.0	Bool	cablated normally open
"limit_switch_gate_close"	%I0.2	Bool	cablated normally close
"limit_switch_gate_open"	%I0.1	Bool	cablated normally close
"mem_command"	%M0.0	Bool	mem command pressed
"Safety photocell"	%I0.3	Bool	cablated normally close

Observe the contact "Limit_switch_gate_open", on the functional diagram it appear close (therefore with the old static nomenclature N.C.), it is inserted in the Network 1 in N.O. according to the old nomenclature, finding justification in the Gottardo rule.

This command sets a bit in the merker area, at Bit 0 of Byte 0.

The contact of this coil bypasses the manual command making the signal self-retained.

It is a good rule not to act immediately in the motors but to memorize the events with the same effect to avoid command conflicts.

Network 2: delay after command botton and movent of 3sec

Symbol	Address	Type	Comment
"mem_command"	%M0.0	Bool	mem command pressed

The memory of the opening command, located in the marker M0.0, controls this timer with delay excitation action, TON.

The PT value is set in millisecond, so 3000, and the instance DB is hand renamed "pre_movement_3s", inside it there are the bit ".Q" usable like digital timeout signal.

It is necessary to observe the number of the instance DB because this will be used for manual accesses, for example to switch on a pilot light in the HMI interface.

Network 3: open gate contactor

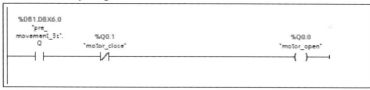

Symbol	Address	Type	Comment
"motor_close"	%Q0.1	Bool	close gate contactor
"motor_open"	%Q0.0	Bool	open gate contactor
"pre_movement_3s".Q	%DB1.DBX6.0	Bool	

The first boolean signal is on instance data block, DB1, to the seventh byte, first bit, in fact the offset numbering always starts from the zero address.
This segment implement the interlocking between the hardware commands sent to the motor run contactors.
forward run is allowed if the backward is not in progress.
In the fourth segment we note a parallel of conditions followed by a Boolean in series that has the effective control of the blinking generation.

Network 4: Alert, gears will move

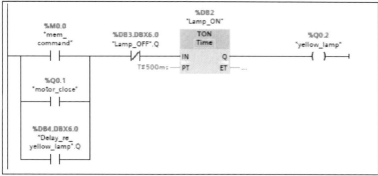

Symbol	Address	Type	Comment
"Lamp_OFF".Q	%DB3.DBX6.0	Bool	500ms Lamp Off, 1Hz
"yellow_lamp"	%Q0.2	Bool	Alert, gears will move
"mem_command	%M0.0	Bool	mem command pressed
"motor_close"	%Q0.1	Bool	close gate contactor

The square wave needed to flash the yellow lamp, at the frequency of one Hz, is generated using two timers, mutually controlled by the crossed digital outputs.
The invert of "Lamp_OFF.Q" contact is initially high because the PLC at the STOP-> RUN transition performs a total reset of the PAA (IPO) and PAE (IPI) process image areas as well as timers, counters and merkers.

The rule is to warn the users, with three seconds in advance, that mechanical organs are about to start moving.

The flashing signal remains even during each movement.

Network 5 does not implement the half-period, as it might seem from the PT setting in milliseconds.

Only a trigger signal, one millisecond long, that causes the previous timer to restart will be present at output "Lamp_OFF.Q".

Network 5: Yellow lamp logic control and OFF clock Alert

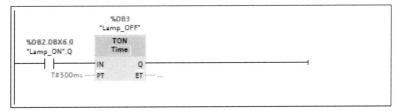

Symbol	Address	Type	Comment
"Lamp_ON".Q	%DB2.DBX6.0	Bool	1 Hz lamp OFF

At this time of the sequence, as also shown by the functional diagram, the mobile part of the gate is traveling, until it intercepts the "limit_switch_gate_open".

it is necessary to activate two Timers that will continue in parallel, but the first will activate the flashing 3 seconds before the inversion.

Network 6: Yellow lamp logic control and ON clock (warning gate is going to close)

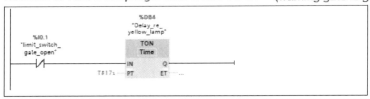

Symbol	Address	Type	Comment
"Delay_re_yellow_lamp".Q	%DB4.DBX6.0	Bool	
"limit_switch_gate_open"	%I0.1	Bool	cablated normally close
"mem_command"	%M0.0	Bool	mem command pressed
"motor_close"	%Q0.1	Bool	close gate contactor

Network 7: yellow lamp 1Hz, gate is closing

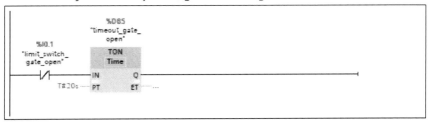

Symbol	Address	Type	Comment
"limit_switch_gate_open"	%I0.1	Bool	cablated normally close

The Delay_re_yellow_lamp timer takes care of pre-warning the users.
It is set at 17 seconds, while the "timeout_gate_open" timer set at 20 seconds, generates the command useful for the self-holding segment of the closing movement.

Network 8: close gate contactor

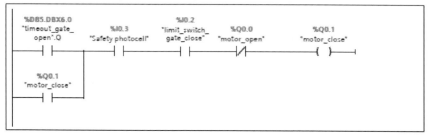

Symbol	Address	Type	Comment
"motor_close"	%Q0.1	Bool	close gate contactor
"motor_open"	%Q0.0	Bool	open gate contactor
"limit_switch_gate_close"	%I0.2	Bool	cablated normally close
"Safety photocell"	%I0.3	Bool	cablated normally close
"timeout_gate_open".Q	%DB5.DBX6.0	Bool	

The "Safety_photocell" performs a self-latching release, as well as the "limit switch gate close", and are therefore subject to the Gottardo rule, which requires the display to be reversed with respect to the functional.

The interlocking contact, "motor_close" appears in the same state as the functional diagram as it is not responsible for releasing the self-latching.

If the safety photocell is interrupted, the effect is also reflected in the first segment of the program.

Observing at the central parallel branch it is clear that it is formed by the logic "inversion of the safety photocell & limit switch gate close".

When this branch is true, it replaces the normal manual command, then the delay of three seconds is triggered before opening the gate.

This is the normal basic cycle. Now you need to debug that is done with the online system.

It is not important with which CPU the automation has been implemented, now it is necessary to check that the system is online.

A simple color code shows us if the offline version, residing in the PC, is the same as in the PLC site.

The orange color was chosen to indicate that the PLC or some other part of the system is online.

The green color in the segments shows the energized parts.
It must be clear that the segments in Step 7 do not represent an electrical scheme but rather a logical sequence.

Only one chain of TRUE, from the vertical line on the left to the load brings the coil to the high logical state.

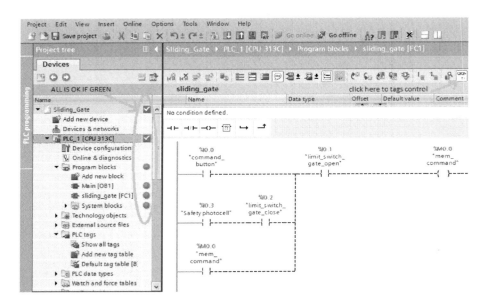

A complete debug must be carried out on the entire cycle then on all segments.

The basic rules of programming must be respected, for example there must not be two calls with a simple reel of the same exit point.

The three-story elevator program explains how to collect functions that perform the same action, such as the uphill sensor, on intermediate markers.

Then inserted in a parallel logic they will act only once in the physical output, for example% Q0.0

If this rule is not respected only the last instance of the output under examination will act while the previous ones are ignored.
No syntax error is indicated by TIA Portal.

The HMI and WinCC.

The HMI panel programming software, WinCC, is available in three versions, Basic, Comfort and Advanced Professional.

Often the didactic laboratories are equipped with the Basic version because it is cheap and inserted into the starter kit.

Students suffer severe limitations because many things are not possible with Basic version.

The automatic gate animation can be done in two ways.
1. Page change on trigger signal.
2. Image selection within a graphic list.

WinCC is fully integrated in the TIA Portal so selecting from the project tree of a screen's drawing area involves switching to the WinCC environment.

The three images shown here are available on the website www.gtronic.it for easier reproduction of the exercise proposed here.

Observe the flashing yellow signal, the drawing art must be superimposed with a WinCC object, for example a pilot light. The three images are available in the PLC programming section of the gtronic.it site

On the CPU properties of the project tree enable the flashing bit at a frequency of 1Hz.

```
           %M100.5                              %Q0.2
          "Clock_1Hz"                    "yellow blinking
                                              lamp"
    ├──────┤ ├──────┬───────────────────────( )──────────┤

                                           %DB1.DBX0.6
                                          "HMI_Variables".
                                           HMI_Yellow_
                                          blinking_lamp
                    └───────────────────────( )──────────┤
```

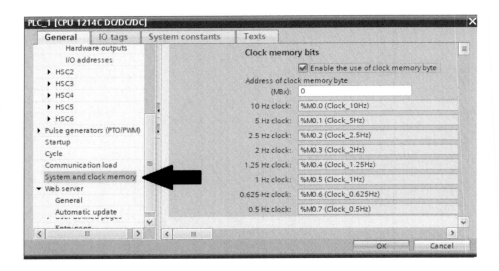

The graphic list

A graphic list is a technique that allows you to create a unique container for a quantity of related images in a context.

It is possible to simulate animations controlled by the status of preselected variables.

The control variables can be Boolean, allowing the selection of only two states to be represented, for example a close gate and open gate, or integer so as to allow more refined animations.

In the domotic gate control program we can represent 3 states, 0 = gate is close, 1 = gate in motion, 2 = gate open.

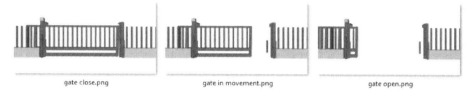

gate close.png   gate in movement.png   gate open.png

The collection of the three images must be inserted in the correct sequence in the Text and graphics list menu, in the HMi section of the project tree.

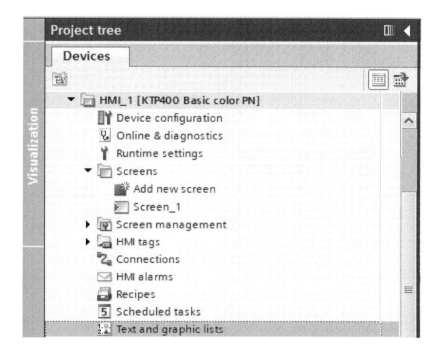

The system is positioned in the text list area, so it is necessary to move by clicking on the indicated tab.

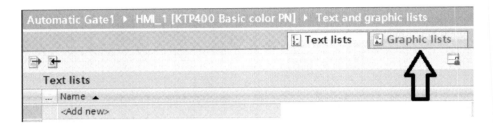

You must create and name for the graphic list. In this case, one is enough but a synoptic of normal size will have several dozen of animate graphics.

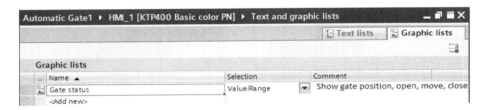

Drag any images, drawn with Paint, or taken from libraries, in specific positions.
It is also possible to integrate images simply with cut and paste.

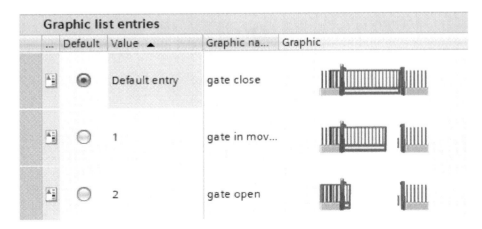

The zero value, indicated as default entry, must be set because in case of loss of communication with the control system one of the images is shown, in our case the gate is closed.

The graphic list must now be inserted in the area of the main page of the HMI.

We aim with the mouse at the point shown in the image, right click, copy.

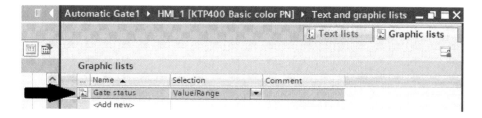

In the graphic area of the main screen we perform "Past", as shown in the figure.

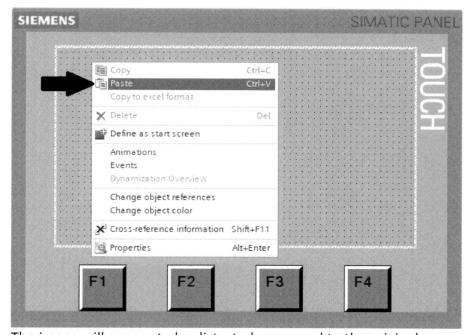

The image will appear to be distorted compared to the original.

Don't worry, you will just have to point with the mouse on the small square on the right and perform the stretch until you get the size of the complete coverage of the graphic area.

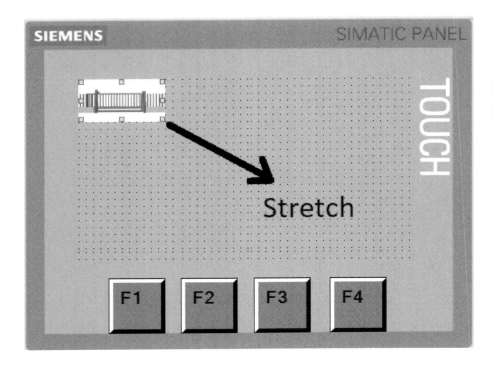

The graphic list must be placed in the background of the area, so that we can position other WinCC control and command objects, for example command buttons, pilot lights, text lists, etc.

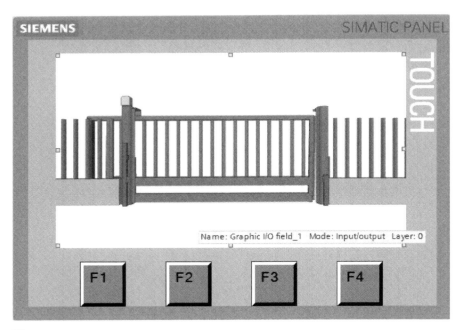

With the right click, call the command "Order" and so "bring to front".

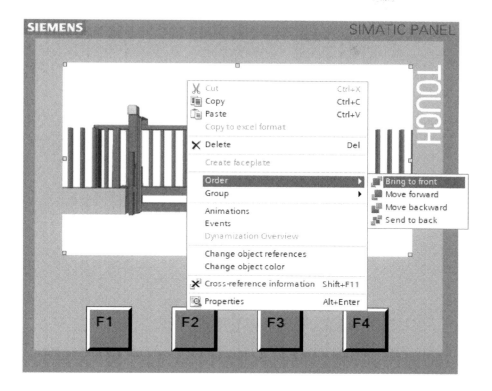

Now that the graphic list is ready you need to check the variable to which it refers so that you can select the three images it contains.

The control variable must be placed in the global data block.

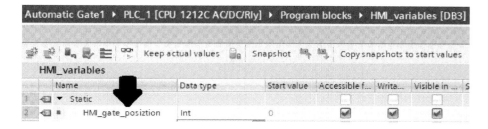

Step 7 segments must be programmed to make this variable assume the value corresponding to the desired image at the appropriate time of the automation cycle.

0 will be placed in the variable if the automation is at machine zero.

This is true when the closed gate limit switch is intercepted.

It is set to 1 in the variable when at least one of the motor's travel directions is active.

It is set 2 when the gate open limit switch is intercepted.

Here's how to add these networks into the existing gate control program.

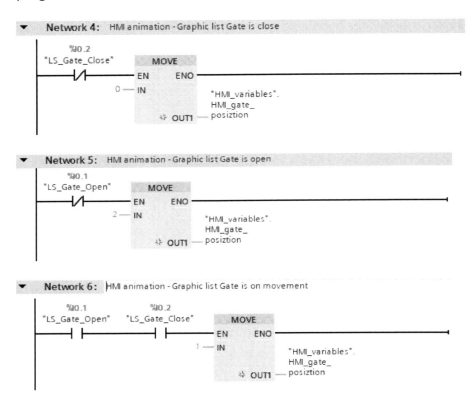

The faceplate.

Faceplate is a technic that allow to represent a common control panel for an object present in multiple item in the same plant.

For example a faceplate can be an inverter control panel or simple a motor parameterization that indicate torque, rpm, nominal supply voltage or ampere at the nominal cos ∅.

The generation of faceplate is suggested for the comfort or advanced HMI panel and is not available for the basic one.

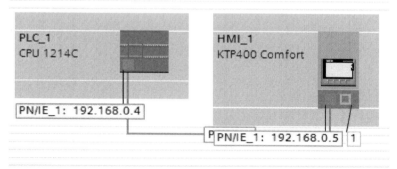

The topics related to the faceplates are:

- Releasing the faceplate
- Updating faceplates
- HMI user data type (HMI UDT)
- PLC data types

Faceplates consist of a compilation of display and operator objects like pilot light, emission immission field, etc, which can be manage and modify centrally in a library.

Storing the faceplates in a library enables re use them easily in different projects.
The building of faceplate start drawing a simple rectangle in the design panel area.

Open the first screen in the HMI WinCC Confort or Advanced editor.
Draw inside the area a rectangle and place inside it all the object that we want replicate in any instance of the face plate.
In our case we have a motor control that need speed up speed down button, imission field for numeric speed expressed in RPM and a current limit protection.
An analogic gauge can express the max temperature tolerated by the inverter
In the image below is shown the basic construction of faceplate.

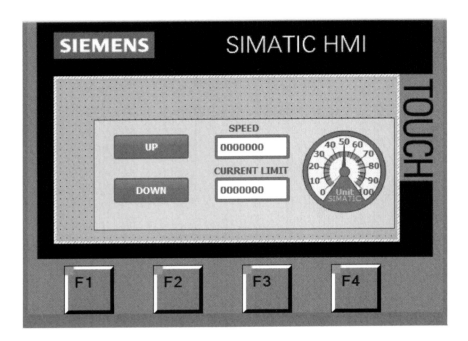

Next step is to create from this simple draw a unique entity interconnected to a variables that is not directly allocated in a global data block.

Right click on the middle of rectangle, act on create a faceplate.

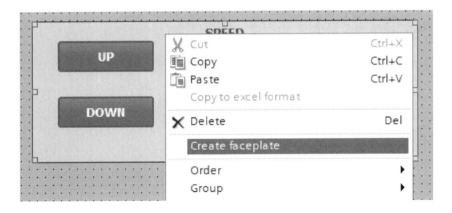

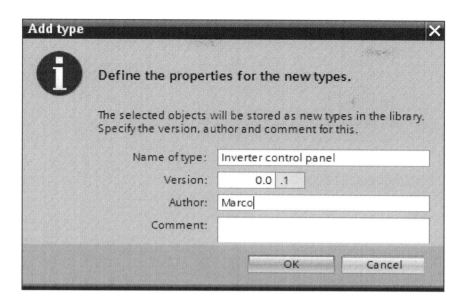

In the next step we have to interconnect local object in the faceplate to the property local variables.

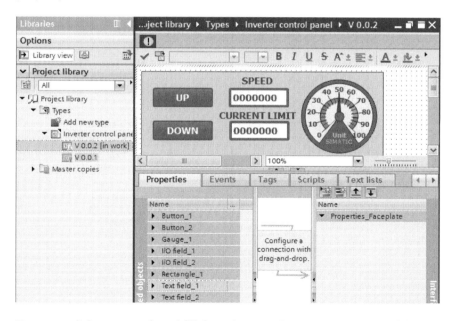

Next step click on tags tab and fill the value creating same names variables.

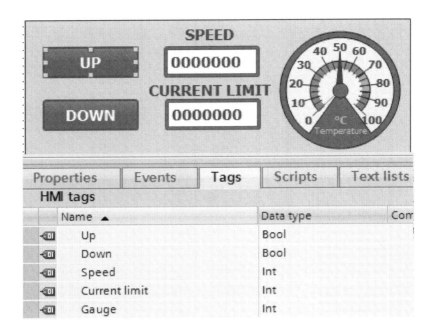

Every expert programmer must know "pop-up of the face plate" technique in order to make front panels common to many identical devices easy to use without having to rewrite the same code with multiple repetitions.

Generate a pop-up using faceplate, double click to "Add new pop-up screen" to create a pop-up with a name

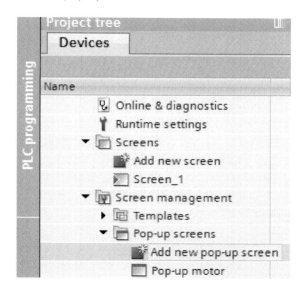

Drag & drop faceplate from project library to pop-up screen and resize the pop-up screen using property\layout path.

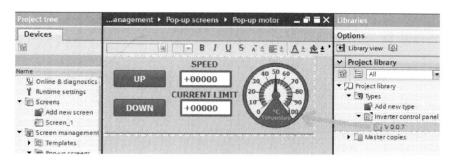

Generate a Graphic lists using for example a motor image from Toolbox\Graphics\Automation\Motors path

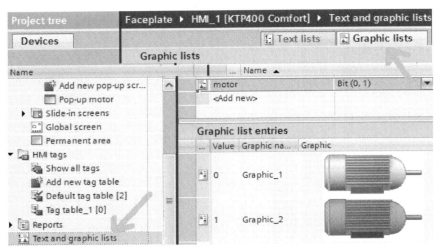

Drag & drop Graphic list into main screen

It is a good technique to superimpose a gived transparent property button on the graphic list, acting on its properties.
Run the "group" command so that the object becomes unique and indivisible inheriting all the characteristics assigned to each component of the group, including the variables and the way in which they act.

How to upload the program from the PLC

For PLC versions prior to firmware 40, the procedure for recovering a program from a PLC memory, in a TIA PORTAL V15 environment, is not as easy as it was in the old Simatic manager.

In some particularly unfavorable conditions it may not even be successful.

The system can almost always guarantee a partial recovery which then requires manual intervention, for example by adding the hardware sections not reached by the automatic procedure.

Rule 1 - The download of the program from the PLC memory is complete if it contains hardware and software. Hardware means that models and configurations are also downloaded for any expansions.

Rule 2 - The procedure is successful if the firmware Siemens identifies firmware 4.0 or higher, for example 6ES7 "40" and not 6ES7 "31".

While in new firmware versions it is sufficient to download the object as a "new station".

After each back up maneuver it is a good idea to check that everything has actually been unloaded.

The first versions of the 1200 series CPUs had the firmware indicated with 30.

Obviously today they are no longer on the market but it might be possible to find them in first-generation systems.

It is possible to update the firmware of these CPUs, but it is possible to lose the program they contain.

To perform the update you need an original Siemens SD card, size 24 Mbyte, in which the firmware released on the official website has been loaded. Do not attempt to use a normal SD card.

The reading of PLCs with archaic firmware will be possible only with TIA PORTAL version 11 rare today to find.

First condition - CPU with firmware 4.0 prior.

Create an empty project in which the CPU of our interest has been manually entered. 6ES7 212-1BE31-0XB0

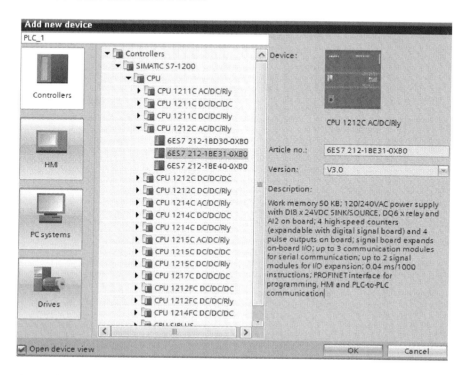

Once the station is inserted, a Profinet subnet must be added and assigned the IP that is indicated in the P&ID.

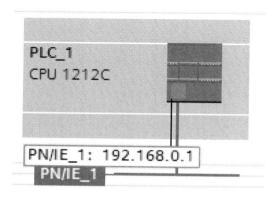

Let's go online, all accessible stations will be shown.

When trying to download as a "new station" from online, this message is returned for 31 for V3.0 models that do not support downloading.

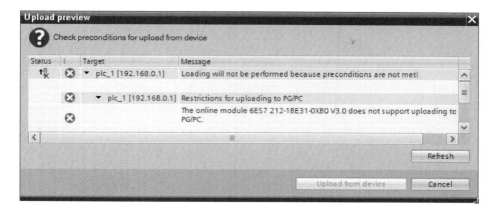

We go online, acting on the canonical key, the network is first interrogated and then the station declared off-line is detected.

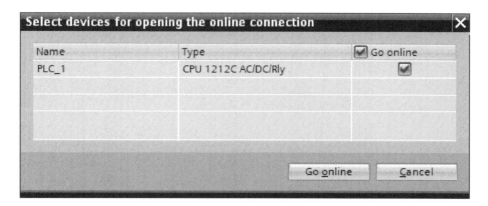

If we are in a plant context, all compatible devices will appear, ie all PLCs.

Select the one from which want to extract the program and bring it online.

Press the "GO online" button.

Following another path we could see the window shown in next image appear.

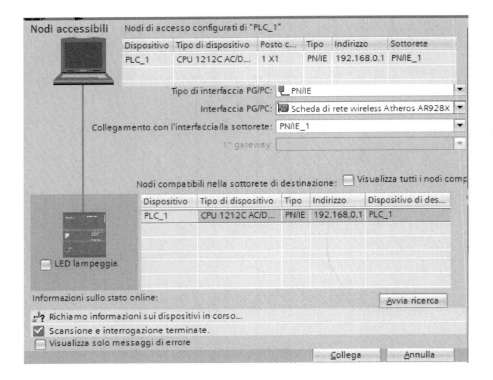

Click on "GO Online".

Going online the window shown below appears, which obviously warns that the offline program is different from the online one.

This technique will have the serious defect of not being able to recover the hardware configuration.

Only firmware V4.0 on PLC 40 can delivery all hardware configuration incluse the espansion blocks.

The most important thing is that the Upload button is active, as shown in the next image.

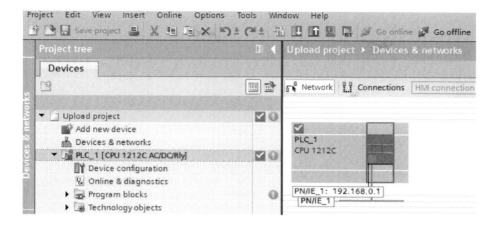

The orange dots indicate where the difference between the online version and the offline version was detected.

The goal is to have only green dots next to each block or sensible element of the project tree.

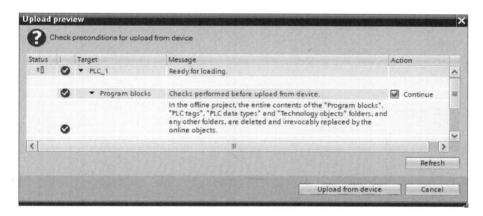

Once you have reached the window shown, check "Continue" and press the "Upload from device" button.

The download will begin, with a duration proportional to the number of objects to be recovered and their extension.

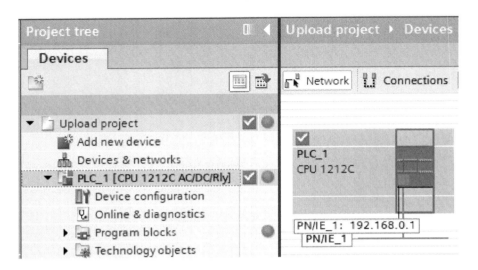

The present of dots and green cues indicates what has been downloaded and now coincides in version between online and offline.

Saving is essential, otherwise the recovered program will not be present at the next opening.

To verify that the program exists on the PC hard disk, disconnect from the system, "Go offline".

Open the Tags table to verify that these have been downloaded together with the blocks of code Step 7.

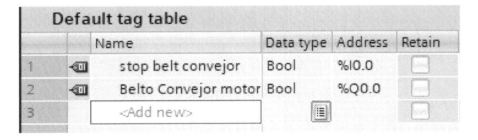

Open the blocks to have the final confirmation that the program has been fully registered.

The following section presents the automatic method for downloading the program including the hardware configuration.

Obtain the system hardware configuration wen firmware 40 or above.

The configuration of an entire system, which is online, can be downloaded directly including all the modules contained in the project as long as it is a latest-generation CPU or frimware 40 or higher.

We must proceed by creating a new empty project, to which we assign the desired name, and in which we select "CPU not specified".

It is also possible to completely skip the hardware configuration by going to portal view -> First Steps -> Create PLC Program. In this way, TIA Portal still selects the CPU not specified as shown in the figure.

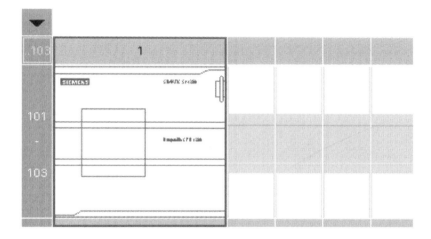

Continue by selecting the "Hardware Detection" command from the "Online" menu.

The system starts detecting the CPU and the SM expansions, that is the digital or analogue I / O expansion modules, SB signal board and CM communication modules, these will be placed in the left slots on the CPU.

Notes: it is possible to configure the CPU to obtain particular behavior when restarting and / or charging a program (entire project) or updating data blocks or functions.

In the second case it is possible to update the program without resetting the current plant production cycle.

It is possible to configure, by acting on the properties of the expansion block, the individual inputs, for edge signal detection and "pulse measurement" (so that after an instantaneous impulse they remain active). configure the outputs so that there is a change from RUN to STOP they use a freezing value or a substitute value.

Setting up retentive memories .

When the control unit is restarted and/or during changes in operating status, the internal variables are generally reset.

This can cause danger situations if some settings have to be reintroduced by the operator or even represent personal or duty enjuring situations. Consider the case of hanged loads.

In some cases, the security or the system logic dictates that the settings of the variables prior to the restart or abnormal situation be remembered as rebooting and not reset.

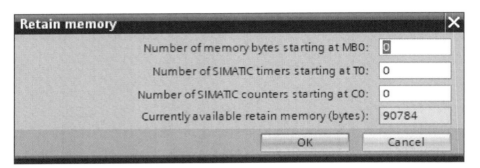

To set or change the areas to be retentive, in the context of our project access is gained from within the default tags table using the button that shows the wrench icon.

All PLCs are able to provide the user with the configurability of the memory retention area.

Only in the old Step 5 versions these were preset in the factory, therefore not movable or assignable by the user.

How to Backup an HMI.

In this exercise we learn the procedure for backing up an active HMI in a plant.

The direct and software procedure is not easy and may require complex maneuvers with additional software.
Previous versions of WinCC, for example released in 2008, backed up the entire program and its components without problems.

To perform a hardware backup, safe and effective, today it is sufficient to use a USB support, in the appropriate port of the panel, and in the boot phase, recall the back up function in the mass storage unit.

To save the entire program, including the HMI operating system, follow this procedure.

The major shortcoming of this method seems to be the impossibility of modifying parts of the program in the editor.
The backup is carried out in a monoblock format, useful to be reloaded in another panel or archived.

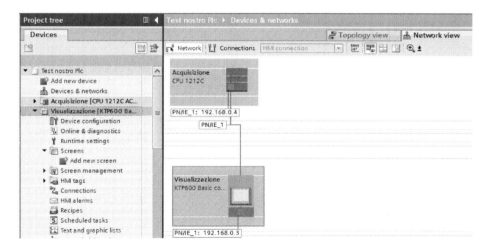

The first step consists in inserting in the project tree an HMI equal to the existing one.

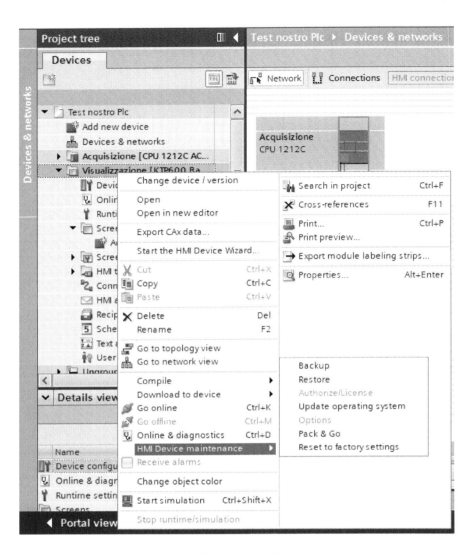

Then, on the project tree, right-click on the HMI Device maintenance, so select Backup.

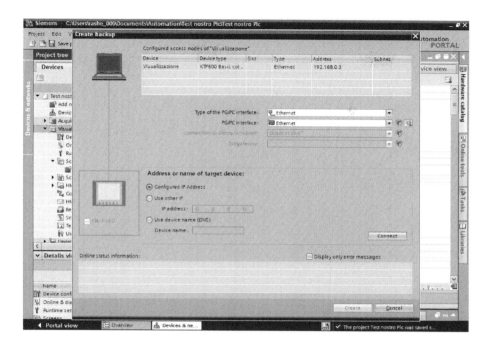

Check that the communication is set and set with the Ethernet protocol. Establish the connection by clicking with the left mouse button on Connect and then create.

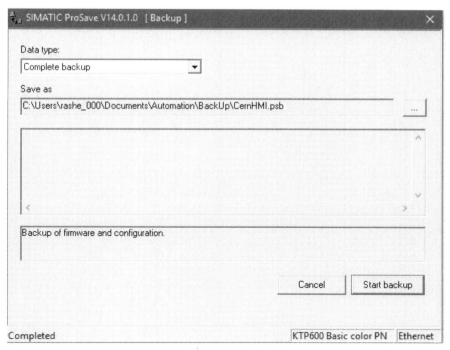

Choose the output folder by clicking with the left mouse button on three dots (next to "Save as")

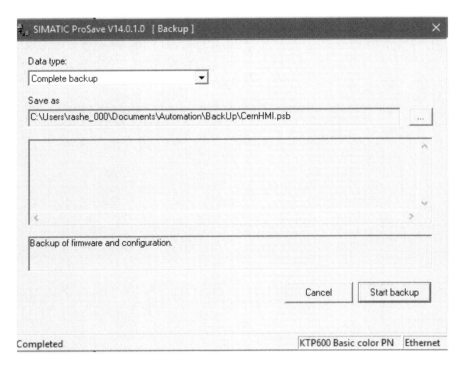

Step VII Click "Start backup" with the left mouse button and wait for the end of the procedure

Procedure for uploading an HMI

Right-click on the drop-down menu and click on HMI Device Maintenance

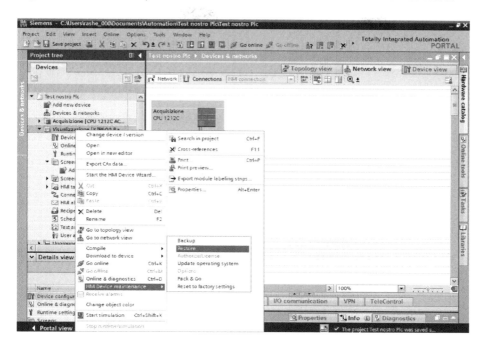

Press the left button on "Restore"

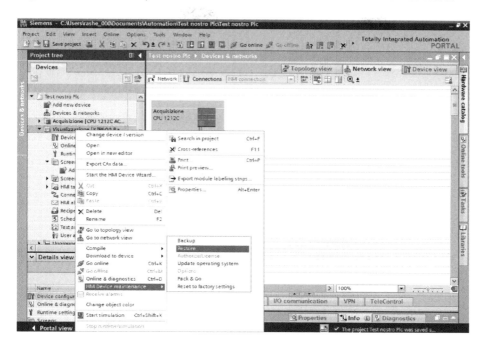

Exercises

Optimized combinatorial networks.

Combinatorial logical networks are often synthesized starting from a truth table, but sometimes also starting from a Boolean logic function.
There is almost always a way to reduce this function to an equivalent one that involves the use of a smaller number of elements.
These elements can be indifferently concrete as electromechanical relays as or software.
While a minimized electrical or electromechanical circuit has a definitely lower cost than that realized in brute, an optimized software will present a greater speed of execution and less heaviness for the CPU that must execute it.
We see a simple example with a function of only 4 input variables.

$$y = \overline{AB}\,\overline{CD} + \overline{AB}CD + \overline{AB}\overline{C}D + \overline{A}BCD + A\overline{B}\,\overline{CD} + A\overline{B}CD + AB\overline{C}D + ABCD$$

This can be represented, through a truth table having a one logical in the output column in correspondence of the addends that appear in the function, for example the first would be 0000 the second 0011 the third 0101 etc.,
obviously keeping the columns sorted starting from the left ABCD. The table is therefore:

A	B	C	D	y
0	0	0	0	1
0	0	0	1	0
0	0	1	0	0
0	0	1	1	0
0	1	0	0	0
0	1	0	1	1
0	1	1	0	0
0	1	1	1	1
1	0	0	0	0
1	0	0	1	0
1	0	1	0	0
1	0	1	1	1
1	1	0	0	1
1	1	0	1	1
1	1	1	0	0
1	1	1	1	1

The truth table is obtained, respecting the weights of the BCD code 8421, ie the least significant change of state at each line, the second every two, the third every 4 and the last, that is the leftmost every 8 lines.

The karnaugh map represents the same table but so that adjacencies or unit distances can be respected, therefore the variation of at most one bit in passing from one configuration to the next.

This allows to mask through common actions of the boolean algebraic factor common gatherings.

We should also take into account some principles and theorems that are valid in a specific way for Boolean algebra, for example a bit added to the denied of itself is always 1.

This situation is called tautology.

Let's look at a simple example.

$$y = \overline{A}\overline{B}\overline{C}\overline{D} + A\overline{B}\overline{C}\overline{D}$$

We can easily see that we can collect the inverted terms (not B, not C, not D) in a common factor, obtaining:

$$y = (\overline{A} + A) \cdot \overline{B}\overline{C}\overline{D}$$

Since the first factor is a tautology, it can be replaced with the following:

$$y = 1 \cdot \overline{B}\overline{C}\overline{D}$$

Given that 1 is the neutral element of the product we can say the initial expression is equal to the negative of the three BCD variables,

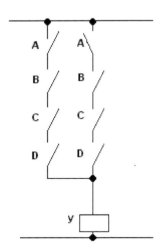
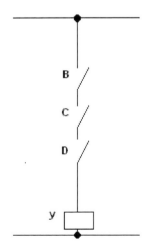

The Ladder segments transform from this:

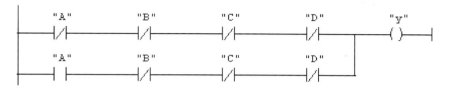

To this:

More complete and complex the truth table is, the greater the simplification achieved.

The karnaugh map is designed so that it can maintain adjacencies between one configuration and the next of the empty and standard truth table according to the 8421 weights.

A planar representation of a mathematical object is obtained which from the adjacency point of view is spherical, in fact the sides must be closed again on themselves, they must carry out adjacency in the transition then the change of state of at most one bit.

To achieve this we should represent, in an ordered manner, two variables as indices and the other two column indices. It result.

AB \ CD	00	01	11	10
00	1	0	0	1
01	0	1	1	0
11	1	1	1	1
10	0	0	0	0

Observe at the bits that are in the adjacency of the high logic state, we have identified a map in the center of the karnaugh map, which permit the elimination of two variables, a quadruple adjacency in correspondence of the third line and an adjacency to the marginal boxes of the first row. The adjoining variable that changes state is eliminated.

The sub-map in the center activates output y only when inputs B and D are present in hight state.

In the submap. in the third row only CDs remain constant while AB are eliminated from the function expression.
The first and last cell of the first row mean that the output y is activated when BCDs are in low state.
The minimized function remain:

$$y = BD + CD + \overline{B}\,\overline{C}\,\overline{D}$$

Which is implemented with the next Ladder segment.

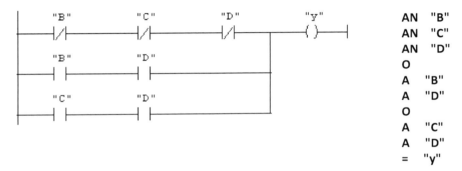

It is left to the reader, as a useful exercise, to develop the combinatorial logic network not minimized so that it can be compared with the one shown above

Semi Automatic belt conveyor with wrenches counter .

A long conveyor belt connects two factory departments that produces wrenches.

The worker on the right performs a quality check of the wrenches taken from the transit warehouse to the deposit. This worker has a conveyor belt control console.

In the control console there is only the system start key, a button, wired normal 0 pressed 1, which restarts the tape, a yellow blinking lamp to signal that the tape is in motion.

When the "restart" button is pressed, the conveyor starts and remains in motion if no more than 20 seconds have elapsed between two wrenches if the counter has counted 4 wrenches.

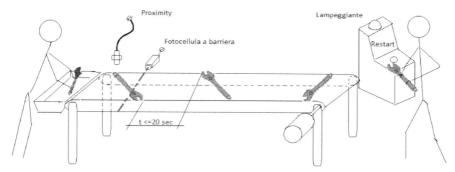

The conveyor stops even if the optical intrusion barrier is interrupted, or by removing the system ignition key from the console.

If the conveyor stops for Time-out between two keys, when restarting,

The worker received the wrenches in groups of 4 and forms the packages containing this number.

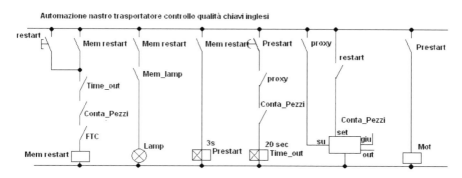

The functional diagram provided is left to the reader for the implementation of the STEP7   segments.

Appendix.

This section lists the main types of sensors and actuators available on the market.
The electrical and hardware features are shown for quick use with the PLC.

Pre-amplified single-point load cells

The load cell, shown in the photo, is widely used as a sensor in scales with a weighing plan of size 400x400mm.
It is produced by a well-known Italian company **Laumas** which is conquering the national market.
It can be powered directly through a wide range of voltage from 12V to 30V D.C.

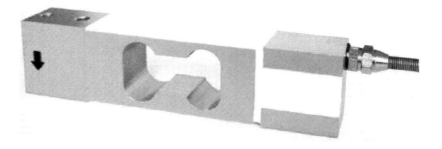

This device does not require additional electronics interface , it is powered and directly connected to the PLC analogue input in the 0..10V range.

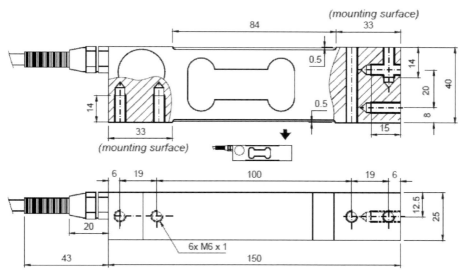

The load cell is substantially a spring coupled to a strain gauge is designed to measure forces of the order of Kg (with grams resolution), quintals and tons. It is acquired as a unipolar or bipolar analog signal depending on the case. The sensor is usually inserted in a resistive bridge circuit whose branches can be compensated in zero and field.

Often the bridge is combined with a differential instrumentation amplifier made with operational amplifiers in differential configuration.

The shape of the load cell body allows it to work both in traction and compression.

Strain gauge combinations can also detect elastic deformations of mechanical systems such as beams etc.

Networks of these sensors can define stress matrices on a structure allowing the study of finite elements.

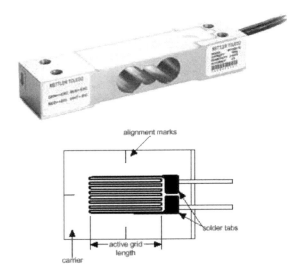

These load cells can be acquired by a PLC once they are connected to a signal conditioner, for example a scale produced by the Laumas, a famous italian company.
The signal can be transduced in analog proportional, in voltage or in current, or be transmitted by the same scale in a special variable, using the Profinet protocol (or others).
The value can be used within a global DB.

There are modular scales, which can be combined with the system, that act as an interface between the load cell and the acquisition system, for example those produced by Laumas visible in the image.

They can be assembled in Omega DIN rail inside the electrical panel.

Note the RJ45 connector that allows addressing it and the dialogue with the Profinet protocol. The signals and power supplies to and from the load cells are connected to the green side terminals according to the serigraphs shown on the side of the device.

A zero calibration and positioning operation must be performed. It is important to read the user manual distributed by the manufacturer to understand where the value read is positioned and in what format within the appropriate register.
These scales also provide standardized analogue outputs according to the 4-20mA, 0-20mA, 0-10V, 0-5V, +/- 5V, +/- 10V levels.

Length of connection cables.

This depends on the type of protocol used to transmit the signal, conditioned and amplified by the balance instrument, up to the PLC or control system inputs.

- RS485: 1000 meters with AWG24, shielded and twisted cable.
- RS232: 15 meters for baud rates above 19200
- Current analogue output: over 500 meters with 0.5 mm2 conductor
- Voltage analogue output: over 300 meters with 0.5 mm2 cable

In the software the signal will be acquired with Step7 NORM_X and Scale_X commands for analogical normalization.

Non Siemens Profinet decentralized peripherals .

The decentralized peripherals with the Profinet standard follow the same concepts based on Profibus standards.

The same models were also offered by VIPA, a competing manufacturer of Siemens whose products are fully compatible.

In the image below, a SLIO VIPA model 053 with power supply and expansion modules, follows an example of network insertion.

The expansion modules were supplied in a distributed way through the PMs which discharge part of the bus from the passage of the necessary current.

It is good to think of the inclusion of a PM every 4 or 5 expansion cards the maximum.

When many output blocks are used the current required is greater and the number of expansions to 2 or 3 for each PM in the slots should be reduced.

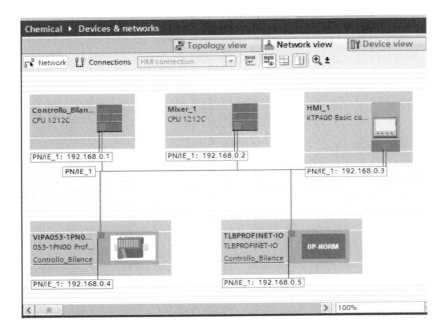

The expansions, mounted on a decentralized peripheral device, act as an extension of the bus, therefore, once the addresses have been detected by querying the properties from TIA Portal, it is possible to pilot an output or read an input as if it were mounted on the main rack.

By this we mean that it is not necessary to use communication protocol commands since these are internally managed.

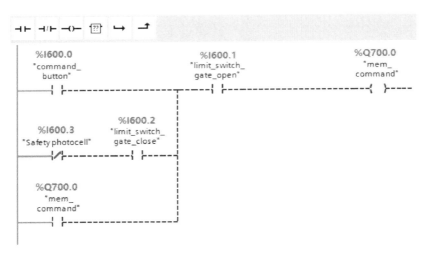

The segment above is an example of how the I / O points available in decentralized peripherals can be managed.

It will make no difference whether it is a VIPA SLIO or a Siemens ET-200.
First of all it is necessary to make the device appear among the devices in network view editor.

In the P&ID the IP addresses of each decentralized peripheral will be reported.

If the SLIO VIPAs are installed, it is also necessary to install the station descriptive files, called GSDs, distributed by the device manufacturer and act as drivers.

These will enrich the TIA Portal V15 hardware catalog.

On decentralized devices, both Siemens and VIPA can be equipped with expansions for the EtherCAT protocol.

In the picture, a VIPA model for EtherCAT.

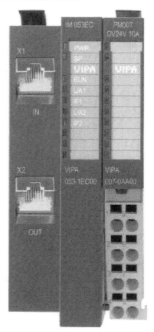

Once the GSD is installed we should insert the new device in the network view. Sometimes it can be difficult to find the new object, the solution is to write the name or part of it in the search bar of the hardware catalog.

When the device is tracked, simply drag it to the network view area. Then we connect the Profinet network between the devices and associate a correct IP.

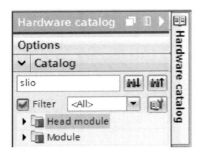

A decentralized peripheral, be it Siemens ET200, or Slio VIPA, or Wago, MURR, Weidmuller, etc. is always composed of the socket, often improperly indicated with "socket", that is the header module, and of the expansion blocks.

The first expansion is a 24Vdc power supply that energizes the subsequent blocks.

The addresses to which the decentralized I / O are accessible are shown by the properties of the object decentralized always in the network view.

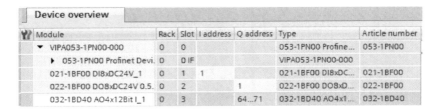

It is clear from the image that the input and output bytes occupy the address 1 that is from% I0.0 to% I0.7 idem for the outputs Q.

As for the analog output channels, these will be CH0 ->% QW64, the next CH1 ->% QW66 etc. up to% QW70.

Sometimes it may be necessary to run% PQW64 indicating direct access to the device instead of through the process image.

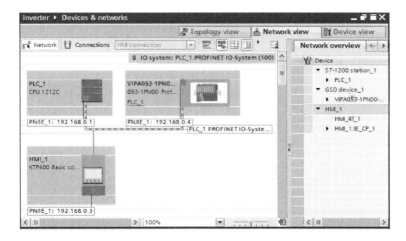

The new elements must appear in the project tree in the ungruped device section

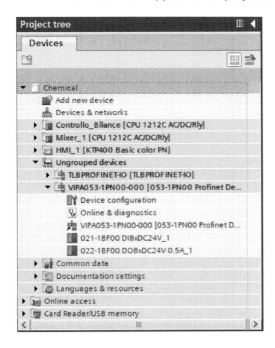

Let's take an example of how to access decentralized peripherals.

Suppose an inverter with analog control is controlled by this expansion.

The net implement a decentralized proportional output control on SLIO.

The constant value 13000 is approximately equal to half of the full scale 27648, therefore in the decentralized peripheral device an analogue output voltage equal to approximately 5V or 25Hz will be generated in the eventual connected inverter.

The motor moves to 50% of the speed indicated on its plate.

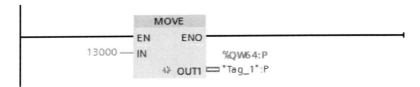

As usual, the address of the analog output terminal is on the device properties, right click on the expansion tree icon on the device tree.

Electromagnetic flow meters.

The electromagnetic flow meters are suitable for measuring electrically conductive liquids. They are distinguished by the type of assembly on the pipes.
Flanged meters are fitted with flanges at the ends connected to the flanges pre-installed on the pipes.
Wafer meters are not equipped with flanges at the end and are enclosed between the flanges pre-installed on the pipes.
Intrusive Meter installation provides that a part of the meter protrude inside the pipe.
The meters can have a separate or built-in converter (compact) that provide a 0-10V or 4-20mA analog signal to PLC.

Nel P&I il regolatore di portata intercetta la tubazione in DN50, generando il segnale elettrico in FZ da inviare al sistema di controllo.

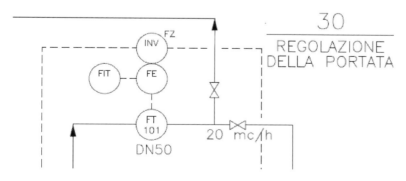

Three rod level gauge.

The simplest and most common level sensor to use is the rod sensor which uses the conductivity of the liquid in which it is immersed to generate one or more ON / OFF signals.
The simplest are two rods, which detect a high or low level alarm, and those with three rods that detect above the minimum and the maximum also the consensus of average, correct, working level, etc.
In the image a three-rod sensor during a test phase.
It is manually immersed in a bucket containing water to check the response sent to the digital inputs of the PLC.

The upper part has an airtight cap that guarantees IP67 protection.
Ensure that the sensor purchased is made of a material resistant to any aggressive agents in which the specific application requires immersion.
The popular 3 rod version allows for 2 levels of detection by a single relay - enabling greater scope for switch based operations. e.g. pump operation - starts on high, stops on low or vice versa for tank filling.

Resistive amplifier relay for level control

A resistive amplifier relay for level control works with the electrical conductivity property of the liquid, detecting the opening or closing circuit between two or three electrodes normally these is the rods of a level gauge.

A complete range of probes and rods are specially designed to answer to all type of applications.

The sensibility is adjusted in relation to the liquid conductivity from 1 to 150 kOhm.

The hysteresis between on/off relay switching is about 10% of sensibility; This is to avoid false alarms originated by smog, foam or condensation of vapours.

With both timers, it is easy to adjust the level detection or level regulation even if the fluid surface is moving (small wave effect).

The typical application is on level control for electrically conductive liquid media:

- Minimal or maximal levels
- Dosing
- flow detection and alarm
- pump control
- solenoid valve control
- fluid detection in a pipe.

With appropriate electrodes for use as limit transducer in:

- Water, wastewater, Acids, lye ,Brines, etc.

Note: One amplifier is necessary for each level to detect.

Operating range

The capacitive resistance of long cables reduces the sensitivity of the electrode controls.

A typical, shielded, 3 conductor PVC cable has a capacitance of approx. 100 pF per meter.

This results in an operating range which is dependent upon cable length and the resistance of the liquid in accordance with the following diagram:

[only for V AC supply]

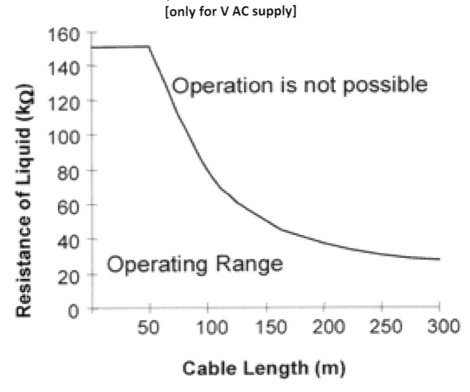

1. ON/OFF Detection: 2 rods

The relay actuates when the liquid allow the current to go through the loop.

2. ON/OFF Regulation: 3 rods

The relay actuates and keeps its function until the liquid reach the upper level (filling) or the lower level (emptying).
A LED indicates the relay status.

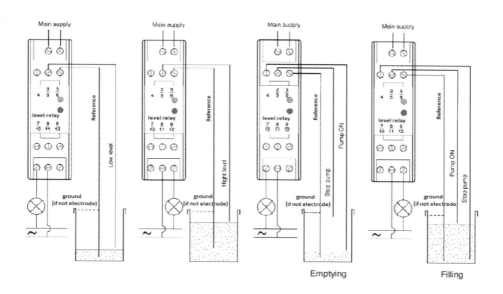

Emptying   Filling

Ultrasonic level sensor Sonar Bero .

The ultrasonic sensors, generally indicated with the term Sonar, cyclically generate ultrasonic pulses which are reflected by even liquid surfaces and objects.

The sensor then determines the distance of the object from the time difference between the emission of the impulse and the reception of its echo.

The sensor detects the distance between it and solid, liquid, granulated or powder materials. The material can be transparent or colored, of any shape with a smooth or rough surface.

Since the sonar exploits the speed of sound waves in the air, temperature, density, and its humidity enter the formula in the form of compensating factors.

For this purpose the best models also incorporate a temperature sensor.

If the sensor is not compensated, it must be taken into account that the reference temperature is 20 °C.

A change in the temperature of e.g. +10 °C determines a variation of the sound wave propagation speed of approximately + 1.75% and consequently a variation on the calculated distance of + 1.75%.

The sensor can work as well as in closed environments, such as for example piezometric wells, tanks, tanks even in a non-closed environment, and normal atmospheric conditions (normal intensity of snow or rain falling in the detection cone) do not affect sensitivity and operation.

Mounting more sonars too close together can create interference in the measurement.

All BERO Sonars with analogue output can be used with 3RS17 series signal converters.

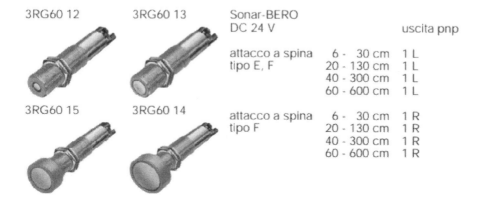

3RG60 12	3RG60 13	Sonar-BERO DC 24 V		uscita pnp
		attacco a spina tipo E, F	6 - 30 cm	1 L
			20 - 130 cm	1 L
			40 - 300 cm	1 L
			60 - 600 cm	1 L
3RG60 15	3RG60 14	attacco a spina tipo F	6 - 30 cm	1 R
			20 - 130 cm	1 R
			40 - 300 cm	1 R
			60 - 600 cm	1 R

The sonars operate in the normal analog ranges 0-20mA, 4-20mA, 0-10V.

The signal conditioners for the acquisition must be normalized.

In TIA environment for S7-300, S7-400, S7-1500 it is possible to integrate in the code the function FC105 , while in the S7-1200 series the pair NORM_X and SCALE_X will be used which are explained in the book dedicated to analogical normalization.

3RG61 12–3..01	Sonar-BERO DC 24 V	uscita analogica 4 - 20 mA	6 - 30 cm	1 L
			20 - 130 cm	1 L
		0 - 20 mA		
	attacco a spina tipo G		6 - 30 cm	1 R
		0 - 10 V	20 - 130 cm	1 R

To acquire and normalize the Bero sonar signals, simply program the Step7 Norm_X and Scale_X sequence.

Example of basic use of Bero sonar

We see, in principle, how to use the compact CPU to measure distances with a Siemens Sonar-BERO of the compact line M18.

The Sonar-BERO emits short ultrasonic impulses in equal time intervals. The time distance between the emission and the arrival of a sonic impulse that was reflected by an object towards the Sonar- BERO is measured and transformed into a frequency.

A rectangular signals appears at the frequency output of the Sonar-BERO whose frequency is proportional to the measured distance. The signal is switched to the Digital input of the integrated counter of the S7 CPU.

The frequency is continously recorded by means of the FB block and is correspondingly recalculated into the according distance in the program itself.

BERO-Contact	Signal Meaning	S7-connections
1	L+	Power supply: +24VDC
2	Enable/Sync	Digital Output: %Q0.0
3	L-	Power supply: M
4	Frequency output	Digital input: %I0.0

To connect a Sonar-BERO with a 1214 DC/DC/DC CPU, a shielded cable with a twisted pair of wires has to be used. (e.g. a PC-Ethernet-connection cable for short distances is very appropriate.)

To ensure a rectangular signal run also for higher frequencies, the output of the Sonar-BEROs has to be strained with a 300 Ohm Resistor (2 W).

If possible, it should be closely positioned to the Digital input of the S7 CPU.

In the operation mode "Frequency measurement", the impulses provided by the Sonar-BERO are counted within the Integration time, thus determining the frequency.

After the completion of the integration time, the measured value is updated.

When exceeding the upper limit or falling below the lower limit, the digital output (%Q0.5) is automatically set.

It is determined via the Hardware Configuration.

In the project tree, right click on CPU icon -> Properties.

Than enable the Hight speed counter

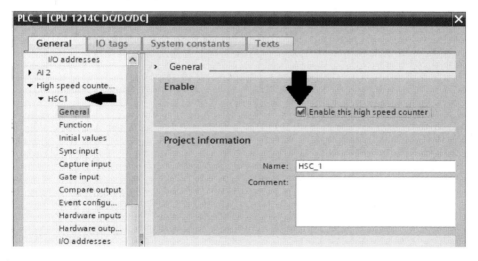

Suppose the used Sonar-BERO has a spanning from the nominal measuring range of 15 cm up to 100 cm.

The frequency generated by the BERO is linear to the distance

In the table is highlight the linear dependence between the frequency returned and the distance between sonar and object.

Distance Sonar-BERO to the object	Generated frequency by the Sonar-BERO
15 cm	150 Hz
100 cm	1000 Hz

The 1kHz frequency makes it impossible to acquire the signal with standard digital inputs because they are subject to the cyclical times set by the IEC61131-3C operating system.

For this reason it is mandatory to use the HSCs.

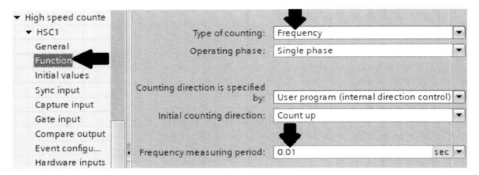

To detect a minimum and maximum level it is necessary to set a higher frequency margin and a lower margin.

In the menù, Hardware inputs, select %I0.0 and the speed of 100kHz sample time (on-board input).

Remember to reduce Digital input filter time ad lower value.

Frequency will be available at the internal address %ID100.

You can use simply comparators to detect in a tank lower and highest level value.

Vibration meter

Vibration monitoring according to ISO 10816, allows an estimate of the machine's life time not only from an electrical point of view but also from a structural point of view.

The measurement unit in Italy is $\left[\frac{mm}{sec}\right]$, while in the UK area countries it is $\left[\frac{inch}{sec}\right]$.

VIBRATION SEVERITY PER ISO 10816						
Machine			Class I small machines	Class II medium machines	Class III large rigid foundation	Class IV large soft foundation
	In/s	mm/s				
Vibration Velocity Vrms	0.01	0.28				
	0.02	0.45				
	0.03	0.71		good		
	0.04	1.12				
	0.07	1.80				
	0.11	2.80		satisfactory		
	0.18	4.50				
	0.28	7.10		unsatisfactory		
	0.44	11.2				
	0.70	18.0				
	0.71	28.0		unacceptable		
	1.10	45.0				

The operating voltage of the sensor is: 18 ... 32 V DC

Provides a switching output: Normally closed DC PNP

The analogue output is often in current: 4 ... 20 mA: measuring range of the effective value: 0 ... 50 RMS mm / s, the frequency range of the vibration that can be estimated is: 10 ... 1,000 Hz,

Often these sensors are exposed outside the structures, therefore subject to atmospheric agents, it follows that the level of protection is at least IP67.

For the electrical connection, an M2 connector is available for this model, while for the mechanical connection: M8 x 1.25

Proximity switch (inductive sensor)

It is a very high diffusion sensor, it is used in all applications where there is no mechanical switching, for example in ATEX place, in environments where dust or paint can solidify inside or on the external parts of the sensor.

Suppose, for example, that a normal limit switch was used in a painting chain, in a short time the vaporized paint, deposited on the external slats, would block the movement and lead to the breaking of the rod.

Looking at the thread of the locking system we could notice that many of these sensors are sealed (GAS thread) which will guarantee a degree of protection up to immersion and / or to IP67 gases.
The operation distance is rather small, about 2mm.

The sensors can have two, three or four terminals.

Those with only two terminals, a blue and a brown wire, which must be connected to L + and the PLC digital input, are often passive and react to the metal masses placed in front of them.

This happens because the mobile part of the internal switch is a magnet that closes on the fixed part because it searches for the external ferrous mass.

It can work with only two wires because inside, the switch slats are inert metal on the fixed one and magnetic metal (a magnet), on the mobile one.

When a metal mass appears in front of the sensor the magnetized lamella, moving, closes the circuit bringing the voltage L + to the digital input of the PLC.

It is a variant of the Reed relay. There are many models of this sensor, whose switching frequency can even exceed KHz, making it possible to detect the cams in a gear wheel.

Variants of this sensor can contain even complex electronic circuits with multiple PNP or NPN outputs. Normally they integrate an LED that shows the switching status.

The sensor diameter is one of the purchase parameters.

Fiber optic detection systems

Fibers for direct reflection
In this type of function the red light emitter and receiver are contained in one fiber (multi cored) or side by side (double cored).

DIRECT REFLECTION   Checking the missing terminals   Checking the form of components

The sensing is obtained by the reflection of the rays of the object to be detected. The parameters that influence the sensing distance are mainly the colour, the reflective or the roughness of the surface to be sensed.
The maximum sensing distances mentioned in the technical characteristics refer to results obtained with a piece of matt white paper dimension 10 x 10 cm.

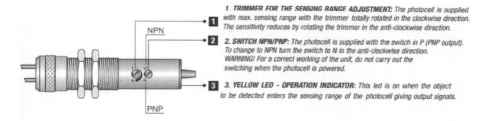

1. **trimmer for the sensing range adjustment**: The photocell is supplied with max. sensing range with the trimmer totally rotated in the clockwise direction. The sensitivity reduces by rotating the trimmer in the anti-clockwise direction.

2. **switch npn/pnp**: The photocell is supplied with the switch in P (PNP output). To change to NPN turn the switch to N in the anti-clockwise direction. WARNING! For a correct working of the unit, do not carry out the switching when the photocell is powered.

3. **yellow led - operation indicator:** This led is on when the object to be detected enters the sensing range of the photocell giving output signals.

N.B. Sensitivity adjustment
• After adjustment the sensitivity can vary depending on variations in the object or conditions in the area of installation.
• As reflection varies in relation to the object, adjustment should be carried out with the object present.
• After having carried out adjustment, the fixing of the way and the curvature of the fiber should not be changed.

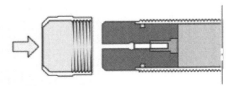

1) Position and screw the locknut in the sensor loosely.

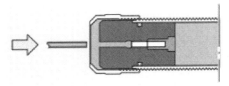

2) With the locknut loose insert the fibers in the two receptacles. Receplacles diameter 2,3 mm

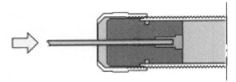

3) With the locknut loose in the fibers ensuring that they reach the end.

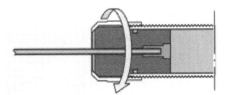

4) Tighten the locknut carefully and ensure that, at the end of the operation, the fibers are blocked.

1 2 3 procedure for the direct reflection fiber optics adjustment: Adjust the sensitivity to minimum turning the trimmer anticlockwise.

Position the object to be sensed at the required distance in relation to the end of the fiber and turn the trimmer slowly clockwise until the yellow led lights up.

Re-check that the calibration is correct by using the object and possibly by repeating the procedure. IMPORTANT: in the presence of objects to be sensed the yellow led should be ILLUMINATED.

Output functions in the absence of the objects to be sensed.

NO OUTPUT = BLACK WIRE (H version = PIN 4)
NC OUTPUT = WHITE WIRE (H version = PIN 2)

Procedure for the thru-beam fiber optics adjustment: Adjust the sensitivity to minimum turning the trimmer anticlockwise. Position the end of the fibers at the required distance and turn the trimmer slowly clockwise until the yellow led lights up. IMPORTANT: in the presence of objects to be sensed the yellow led should be OFF.

Output functions in the absence of the objects to be sensed.
NC OUTPUT = BLACK WIRE (H version = PIN 4) NO OUTPUT = WHITE WIRE (H version = PIN 2)

Encoder

It is an optical type angular sensor that finds applications in positioning problems. The encoder can be of an absolute type or a relative type. Generates a pulse train (incremental encoder) or a combination of pulses for each increase in angular resolution (absolute encoder). The pulse generation speed can be considerable and generally depends on two factors, the number of pulses per revolution and the angular speed of the internal disk. In normal conditions of use it is not possible to acquire the encoder with the normal PLC inputs but we must be connected to the dedicated hardware input in which there is a high-speed counter. The presence of these inputs is checked by reading the data book of the CPU used or purchasing a dedicated expansion block.

Absolute Encoder
- assigns a unique binary code to each axis position.
- does not require zero point calibration.
- uses a particular coding to minimize reading errors.
- the resolution is given by the number of concentric circles.
- manufacturing miniaturization limits the number of concentric circumferences.

Incremental Encoder
- does not assign a unique binary code to each axis position, it supplies square waves.
- it allows to keep track of the displacement of the shaft in clockwise and anticlockwise direction.
- requires zero position calibration.
- it is suitable for high rotation speeds.

Incremental encoders can be constructed in two different ways, with passing or reflected light, in the image we see the internal disk in the two cases.

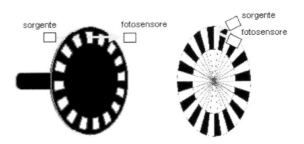

If the encoder has more phases in the disk there are more concentric perforated circumferences which give the output signals shown below with reference to the incremental model:

sens A
sens B
home
sens A
sens B
home

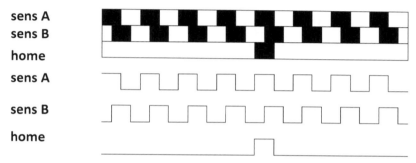

• the zero serves to establish the initial position (home), or to count the lap.
• keeps track of the current position based on the variations of the input of the two sensors.
• the signals generated by the sensors are out of phase by 1/4 of a period.
• by monitoring which is the front that "arrives first" it is possible to establish the direction of rotation.

Sens A: or also phase A, is the reference signal, of rectangular type, is compared with the simultaneous presence or not of the second phase.

Sens B: If this is present simultaneously with phase A, then the moving part is moving forward. If the latter is present alone, then the system is moving backwards.

The detection of the movement direction is delegated to the ExNor logic function followed by the AND function with phase A only.
This logic function is managed by the encoder internal electronics so we should not carry it out with the acquisition system software.

Hardware connection of the encoder to the PLC.

When purchasing the encoder, you immediately realize that there are very variable cost ranges, from € 15 to over € 300.
We must pay attention to effective needs, so as not to throw away money.
Often it does not need a great resolution or a great reliability, other times it is strictly necessary.
It should be noted that not all encoders can be directly connected to the PLC.
The supply voltage must first be checked.
Many guarantee a wide range ranging from 5 to 30V, others instead require a specific voltage, otherwise the device will be destroyed.

Often, the wide range plug-in encoders are of the Open Collector type, therefore they require Pullup resistors to operate.
Quelli che invece dispongono di uno stadio Pusch Pull, saranno alimentabili (dopo un'attenta verifica) direttamente dalle linee L+ e M del PLC, a 24V D.C., e le fasi A/B ecc direttamente collegabili agli HSC del PLC.

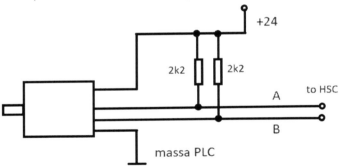

collegamento in modalità Pullup dell'encoder incrementale

Specifiche encoder
We consider one of the most widespread brands to analyze the code that we will find on the body of the device. The brand in question is the Eltra.

The appearance can deceive the student that could be confused with a DC motor reducer or even, by analyzing the outgoing wires with a stepper motor.

on the label appears a coding with as many as 13 elements, almost all of great importance for the technician. Some concern mechanics and installation, others electronics and resolution.

Here is an example.

EL	30	E	500	Z	5	N	4	X	3	P	A	xxx
(1)	(2)	(3)	(4)	(5)	(6)	(7)	(8)	(9)	(10)	(11)	(12)	(13)

Let's see the meaning in detail:

(1)   EL -> Incremental encoder.

(2)   30 -> Diameter of the encoder body, useful for assembling in the chassy of the machines.

(3)   E -> flanges type, other options could be E, H, I or A, B, D, depending on the model.

(4)   Resolution -> is the number of pulses per revolution, in the example there are 500. Possible range 1-> 1024.

(5)   Zero pulse -> there are two possibilities, S = without zero pulse and Z = with zero pulse.

(6)   Supply -> there are two possibilities, S = without zero pulse and Z = with zero pulse

(7)   Output signals -> N = npn, E = pnp, P = push-pull = line driver.

(8)   Axis diameter -> 4 =4mm or 6=6mm.

(9)   Protection lavel -> X = IP54.

(10) Max Speed -> 3 = 3000 revolution per minute (RPM).

(11) P -> Output cable standard length 0.5 meters.

(12) A -> Axial.

(13) XXX -> Special versions coded from 001 to 999, (Manufacturer catalog).

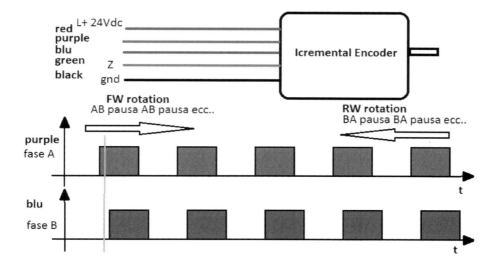

Static relays

The static relays, called SSR or solid state relays, are electronic components that allow to switch the current to a load circuit and provide electrical isolation between the application control circuit and the load circuit.

The static relays appear to be indispensable devices during the production processes that need to activate the load frequently, a feature that concerns most industrial production processes.
They are characterized by a long average life and a low power consumption.

They can be found integrated in industrial thermoregulators or as a discrete component to drive with the digital outputs of the PLC.

For example, it is not possible to use a contactor via the PTO outputs of the PLC, but the problem does not exist for the static relay.

In this way it is possible to implement a PID loop in order to maintain a temperature at the setpoint.

As can be seen from the label it is easy to deduce that the terminals A1-A2, B1-B2, C1-C2, are respectively placed in short circuit when the side terminals are placed a direct voltage between 4 and 32V.
For the maximum switching frequency the databook must be consulted for each model.
However, the voltage is compatible for a direct control of the PLC digital output.

Thermocouples .

It is a non-linear type sensor based on the seebeck effect according to which two metals or two semiconductors, placed in contact and closed in a circuit of suitable morphology, give rise to an electric current.

Opening this circuit we observe a voltage, generally a few millivolts and almost totally devoid of deliverable power, which follows the junction temperature according to a polynomial law linked to the construction materials of the sensor.

Thermocouples in general are not very sensitive and are suitable for measuring temperatures with wide excursions, for example in the steel industry. The seebeck effect has been known since 1821.

The thermocouples are characterized by a letter that indicates the construction materials and therefore the interpolating polynomials. The same letter is combined with a temperature range and therefore a field of use.

Tipo	materiali	Range di temperatura	applicazione
B	platinum-rhodium alloy	0 -> 1820 °C	Iron and steel industry
S	pure platinum-rhodium	-50 -> 1750 °C	Iron and steel industry
R	platinum-rhodium alloy	-50 -> 1700 °C	Iron and steel industry
N	Nickel-chromium-silicon / nickel-silicon	-270 -> 1300 °C	Aggressive environments
K	chromium alloy- aluminum alloy	-180 -> 1300 °C	Obsolete steel industry (Iron)
J	Iron-constantan	-180 -> 800 °C	High sensitivity
T	Copper-Constantan	-250 -> 400 °C	Medium sensitivity cryogenics
E	Chrome- Constantan	-40 -> 900 °C	Amagnetic cryogenics

In addition to the types listed in the table there are other less used ones, for example built with magnetic materials that have been studied for the realization of experimental generators.

It must be emphasized that it is not possible to directly connect the thermocouple to an AD converter because the signal would become extinct due to its natural weakness in power that can be supplied, therefore it must be "conditioned" before being acquired.

The conditioning process consists of a buffering / amplification and subsequent linearization making it transit through a hardware or software network that implements the interpolating polynomial.

It is therefore necessary to specify the type of thermocouple (the letter of the table) to the system in order to be able to linearize using the correct polynomial.

The standard analogue channels are therefore not able to read these sensors unless it is clearly stated in the technical specifications and therefore they have special terminals in which to connect the thermocouple.

Particular integrated cooling circuits are placed behind the specific thermocouple terminals,

for example the well-known MAX31855S and its like whose last letter indicates the interpolating polynomial inside it.

Attention, cables and connectors for thermocouples must be compensated and not just terminals because their presence introduces further thermoelectric effects that strongly unleash the value read.

An input for thermocouples is very different from an input for thermoresistant PT100 since these are instead linear.

To properly set the analogue amplified inputs of the PLC follow the indication:

- TJ -> When a thermocouple is to be connected.
- RTD -> When a PT100 or PT1000 resistors element must be connected.

Visual and acoustic signal tower .

The electrical equipment of automations is regulated, on the installation of an installation, on visual and acoustic signals that the operators in the machine state.

Colors and acoustic signals are regulated in specific countries of installation.

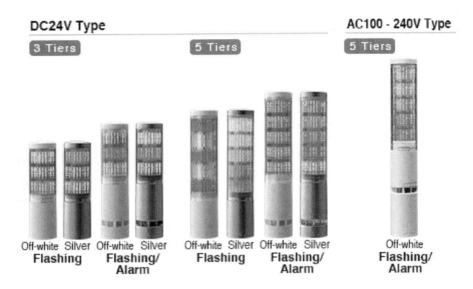

DC24V Type   **AC100 - 240V Type**

3 Tiers   5 Tiers   5 Tiers

Off-white Silver Off-white Silver   Off-white Silver Off-white Silver   Off-white
Flashing   Flashing/   Flashing   Flashing/   Flashing/
              Alarm   Alarm   Alarm

The beginning of each maneuver must be foreseen with acoustic and visual signaling.
A non-blocking operating anomaly must be indicated with a flashing yellow signal combined with the red signal.
A blue signal indicates that a maneuver by the operator is required to reset the system after an abnormal blocker or an alarm.

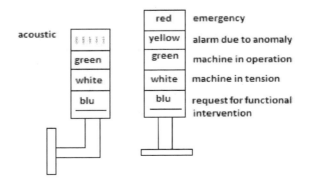

	red	emergency
acoustic	yellow	alarm due to anomaly
green	green	machine in operation
white	white	machine in tension
blu	blu	request for functional intervention

In the image we see the installation phase of the visual acoustic system.

Pilot Light colors and controls, the EN-60073 standard

Red
Meaning: Emergency
Description: Action in danger or emergency condition
Example: Emergency stop command

Yellow
Meaning: Anomaly
Description: Action in case of abnormal condition
Example: Manual intervention to restart an automatic cycle
interrupted, or to suppress an abnormal condition

Green
Meaning: Safety
Description: Operate to set a safety condition
Example: Start command

Blue
Meaning: Obligation
Description: Reset action
Examples: Reset of activated protection relay
Home Machine Request

White - Gray - Black
Meaning: Ordinary maneuver
Description: Action for the general start of functions
except for emergency stop
Examples: Start-up
Listing

Net Switch Profinet.

The Scalance X204IRT is a network switch suitable for applications with PLC networks of the S7-300 / 400 generation and the new S7-1200 / 1500.

It has 4 RJ45 ports and a double 24 V dc power supply.

The Ethernet ports have autonegotiation and autocrossover functions, thus avoiding errors caused by incorrect cabling of the Ethernet network cables, making installation easier for the end user.

The X204IRT ensures excellent performance and maximum compatibility with the most common Ethernet-based protocols and supports all three Real Time classes provided by the Profinet standard, using the "Cut Through" switching mechanism.

It has Web Based Management accessible via broswer or using TELNET, TFTP or SNMP services. In addition to numerous diagnostic and status functions, it is possible:

• set the ports for redundancy in the case of ring connection.
• manage the e-mail agent functionality for sending e-mails containing diagnostic data.
• configure and enable Port Mirroring, which means that data traffic is mirrored by the Mirror Port to the Monitor Port.

A very powerful model of Siemens industrial switch, for mounting on omega rail is shown in the figure.

For the S7-1200 series PLCs it is often used to install an access point (AP) in the same Omega rail, directly in the panel.

Problems due to the shielding of the antenna must be evaluated, since the frame itself is a Faraday cage.

Use only modules designed by Siemens for this specific communication function.

Consult the Tia Portal V15 hardware catalog.

**Scalance
XC-200**

International measurement system.

The international system, indicated with SI, consists of the seven fundamental quantities from which all the others derive. It is universally recognized by scientific communities although other systems such as Anglo-Saxon also exist.

Unit	S.I. unit		Allowed units		relations
length	meter	m			
mass	kilogram	kg	gram	g	1g = 0.001 kg
			tonne	t	
time	second	s	minute	min	1 min = 60 s
			hour	h	1 h = 3600 s
			day	d	1 d = 86400 s
Electric current	ampere	A			
temperature	Kelvin	K	degree Celsius	°C	0°C = 273.15 K
bright intensity	candle	cd			
amount of matter	mole	mol			

Derivative units that have greater interest in the field of industrial automation are shown in the table below.

Unit	S.I. unit		Allowed units		relations
forza	Newton	N			
pressione	Pascal (Newton su m^2)	Pa (N/m^2)	Bar millibar	Bar mbar	1 Pa = 1 N/m^2 1 bar = 100000 Pa 1 mbar = 100 Pa
Lavoro energia calore	joule	J	kilowattora	kWh	1J = 1 Nm
potenza	watt	W			
frequenza	hertz	Hz			
volume	liter	l	Cubic meter	m^3	1l = 1 dm^3 1m^3 = 1000 l

Since in current applications the force is still expressed in kp (kilograms-weight) and the N (Newton) has not yet become commonly used, it should be remembered that the relation exists between the two:

1 N = 0,102 kp   g = 9.81 m/s^2
1 kp = 9,81 N (in via approssimativa 1 kp=10 N)

In the SI system, the force (F) is expressed in N (Newton) and the surface in m^2, therefore:

p = F(strength) / A(surface) = N / m^2 = Pa[Pascal] with equality **1Bar=10^5 Pascal**

note: In Anglo-Saxon units the pressure is expressed in pounds per square inch, (Pounds on square inch) normally shortened, in the scales of manometers, with PSI. (Pound = Libbra).

1 psi = 0,07 bar   **14,5 psi = 1,00 bar**

The thermal powers are expressed in **BTU british thermal units** with equivalence:

1BTU = 1055.05585 joules

Temperature scales for analogical normalization.

The quantities can be measured in multiples and sub-multiples of the various units.

0 K = absolute zero
0 °C = 32 °F ice melting point at atmospheric pressure

- *Kelvin scale: also called thermodynamic scale, is used in physics.*
- *Celsius scale: temperature scale used by most countries. The temperature in degrees*

Celsius is normally called temperature in degrees centigrade.

- *Fahrenheit scale: temperature scale used by some cold countries, where the thermal state of the* of the atmosphere is slightly higher or slightly lower than that of ice.

The use of the Celsius scale would lead to the inconvenience of having to prefix the number with the number temperature, the + or - sign.

Temperature conversion

The temperature variation of 1 degree in the Celsius scale is equivalent to:

- 1 degree variation in the Kelvin scale;
- variation of 1.8 degrees on the Fahrenheit scale.

The conversion relationships are valid:

$$°C = (F-32) / 1,8$$
$$°F = 1,8 × °C + 32$$
$$K = [(°F - 32) / 1,8] + 273$$
$$K = °C + 273$$

Pressure scale for analogical normalization.

The table shows the equivalences between the homologous quantities useful for finding the conversion factors during the Step 7 programming of the analogical normalization blocks

Pressures	kPa	bar	psi	kg/cm²
1 kPa	1	0,01	0,145	0,0102
1 bar	100	1	14,5	1,02
1 psi	6,9	0,069	1	0,07
1 kg/cm²	98	0,0981	14,2	1

To transform i: **kg/cm² in bar o Pa**
It need:
multiply by 105: **1 kg/cm² = 10^5 Pa (100.000 Pa)**

To transform the Pa in kg / cm²
It need:
multiply × 10^{-5}: **1 Pa = 10^{-5} kg/cm² = 0,00001 kg/cm²**

Bibliography

Gottardo, M. (2018, 11 marzo). Let's program a PLC!!!, Edizione 2018. Vigonovo Venezia: Edizioni Gottardo, www.lulu.com.

Gottardo, M. (2018, 11 febbraio). Advanced PLC programming, Edizione 2018. Vigonovo Venezia: Edizioni Gottardo, www.lulu.com.

Gottardo, M. (2018, 29 aprile). Let's Program a PLC!!! Esercizi di programmazione in TIA Portal V15 S7-1200/1500 e PLC modelli S7300-400 WinCC flexible per HMI edizione 2018,Vigonovo Venezia: Edizioni Gottardo, www.lulu.com

Gottardo, M. (20 agosto 2017). Robotica: Basi applicative edizione 2018, Edizione 2018. Vigonovo Venezia: Edizioni Gottardo, www.lulu.com.

Gottardo, M. (2012, 5 settembre). Let's GO PIC!!! The book. Vigonovo Venezia: Edizioni Gottardo, www.lulu.com.

G-Tronic laboratories August 20192019.

Let's GO PIC!!! The book
Marco Gottardo (UK)
ISBN: 978-1-291-06199-4
Complete course, although aimed at beginners, of programming the PIC microcontrollers, on the MpLab platform and Micro-GT hardware. It contains many exercises and examples in Hitech C and Ladder PIC. Examples of use of digital and analog I / O, LED and LCD displays, motor control and serial communication protocols. Great for schools. Three fully completed papers.

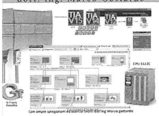

Let's program a PLC (Edizione 2018)
Marco Gottardo
ISBN-10: 172426480X
ISBN-13: 978-1724264800 (Italian)
ISBN-13: 978-1724470249 Advanced
This book, published in March 2018, was created to extend and update the previous edition with the same title published in 2016. It contains the evolution towards the new software platforms and new technologies of PLC and TIA Portal V14 networks. It concentrates the twenty-year experience in the field matured by the author and replaces the previous edition already well known and appreciated by the public. A new layout and the succession with which the topics are presented are optimal both for scholastic learning and for self-learning, bringing them knowledge at a professional level. The text is also suitable for university engineering courses. The use of HMI systems programmed via WinCC integrated in the TIA Portal, connected in Profinet and Profibus completes the preparation of the technician. Each topic is accompanied by numerous exercises. The advanced programming section interfaces a three-phase asynchronous motor to an inverter. The chapter on the normalization of analog signals is fundamental.

Let's Program a PLC!!! Esercizi di programmazione in TIA Portal V15 S7-1200/1500 e PLC modelli S7300-400 WinCC flexible per HMI edizione 2018 Marco Gottardo.
ISBN-10: 1724436465
ISBN-13: 978-1724436467 (Italian)
(English traslation in progress)

This book, published in 2018, is the third updated and expanded edition. Based on TIA Portal V15, it also mentions the previous Siemens versions.

Contains 34 exercises performed, with variants 40.

There are 23 proposed exercises but guided towards the solution.

In the "Professional Projects" section there are 4 professional jobs including one with implementation of the machine self-learning contained in an automatic ironer, the use of HMI systems programmed via WinCC connected in Profinet. Of extreme importance is the underground parking lot that can be converted into an automated warehouse. Equally interesting is a tracking solar panel which shows all the construction phases, mechanics, static energy conversion, PLC control. In the advanced programming section, a three-phase asynchronous motor interfaces with a static converter, inverter, paving the way for all real applications. Unique text of its kind that goes far beyond the normal teaching on the PLC. dr. ing. PhD Marco Gottardo.

Professinonal PLC Programming

Marco Gottardo
ISBN-10: 1729656897
ISBN-13: 978-1729656891

Available on Amazon Book, oriented to the study of industrial processes.
Italian language, imminent translation in English.
Fourth of the complete publication series for school and university. Unique of its kind in Italy.

Let's Build a stereo HiFi
Marco Gottardo
ed. www.lulu.com
(English traslation in progress)

Building HiFi stereo amplifiers is a fascinating field of electronics and thanks to the integrated approach sigle ended with a soft approach even for the beginner. Here are presented many solutions assembled and tested with detailed constructive explanations. The main amplifier is a 40+40Watt built with the ST's TDA2051 with a 5-input mixer, a digital channel selector, preamps with tone control, volume, balance, loudnees filter and 10 + 10 LED VU-meter. You will learn to calculate the RMS power, to distinguish the amplifier class from designing integrated hybrid systems / final power transistors. Among the numerous schemes a powerful 350W amplifier, a home theater system with active filters and 200w sub woofers.

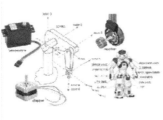

Robotica: basi applicative, edizione 2018
Marco Gottardo
ISBN: 9780244027704
(English traslation in progress)

This book propels us into the fascinating world of robotics, creating the right balance between hobby and engineering science. All the fundamental notions are given or the electronic, mechanical, electrotechnical and programmable logic bases. Some more complex concepts require engineering notions, for example in system programming, therefore they are introduced in a descriptive but still satisfactory manner. The advanced mathematical relations, present at the end of the text, can be learned later when the studies are more mature.
Enjoy your reading and come to the fantastic world of robotics.

Let's Go Pic Essentials: Now
Based on Micro-gt Ide and
Mplab X
(UK)
Available only on Amazon.it
Reduced price compared to the
standard edition, adapted for
high school students.
Blossura: 300 pages
Publisher: Marco Gottardo PhD
Independent Publishing
Platform; 1 edizione (ottobre
2013)
Lingua: English
ISBN-10: 1492851523
ISBN-13: 978-1492851523
Hevy: 862 g

Centro culturale ZIP corso assemblatore di
PC   (English traslation in progress)

Book that introduces to the modern
profession of the technician employed in
computer stores, or installer and
maintainer of multimedia systems. The PC
hardware is placed in the foreground with
an encroachment into the operating
systems, of which an exhaustive history is
also made. The reader will learn to solve
the most common problems, such as the
configuration of a local network, internet
access and the configuration of e-mail.
The chapters dedicated to the settings of
WiFi and the most common peripherals,
printer, are of great importance. fax the
scanner etc.

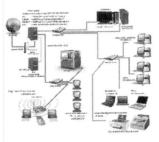

Amministratore, installatore, manutentore delle reti L.A.N

ISBN: 9781291357776   (694 pagine)
(English traslation in progress)

Excellent support for those technicians who have the role of administrator of the servers and systems. The theory is not neglected, as also the technical terminology is seen in the chapters concerning the TCP / IP and the glossary of a beautiful book. The book focuses on the Windows Server 2012 version, but does not neglect previous versions, Windows server 2003 and Windows server 2008, and Windows 8 clients. The chapter on Active Directory is well developed. Extensive exposure of the RAID system

Elettronica Analogica e Digitale con laboratorio e tecniche SMD. Edizione 2017
ISBN-10: 1724826638
ISBN-13: 978-1724826633
(English traslation in progress)
Amazon Book prime
This book, now in its third edition in August 2018, replaces the previous one which improves its graphics and expands some contents. Collects 25 years of teaching experience of the author and offers a wide collection of practical experiences. The reader will be guided in the solution of problems ranging in virtually all fields of electronics. Here you will also find the necessary theoretical bases regarding electronic technology, the development of printed circuits with Eagle, a clear discussion of electrotechnics, strong bases for the use of operational amplifiers, even programmable digital electronics, on PIC Microcontroller systems on the MPLabX platform , an introduction to the development of SoC systems, ie System on chip, is unique in Italy. These are systems based on ZYNQ7000 processors that integrate a powerful multicore ARM section with an extended FPGA area of the Xilinx. An interesting chapter on amateur radio transmissions has been inserted and expanded.

First step on FPGA Xilinx. Introduzione alla progettazione dei sistemi SoC.
ISBN: 9781326806064
(English traslation in progress)

With this publication, the reader will be able to acquire the introductory notions to the FPGA programming techniques currently used in real commercial technology and multimedia products, ie consumer products such as smartphones or game stations, video cameras, biomedical instruments, or niche, for example for the use in real time monitoring, acquisition and control systems used in scientific research.
The devices presented are extremely efficient, integrating powerful processors of the ARM multicore family as well as the latest generation FPGA section, specifically the Xilinx Zynq7000s.

Operazionali 2018 Quarta edizione: Pubblicazioni di Elettronica: Volume 2

ISBN-10: 1724838113
ISBN-13: 978-1724838117

Amazon Prime

This fourth edition, completely renewed in its graphic and revised content, was developed to meet the needs for clarity and synthesis requested by the students of the training courses and hobby courses in the area. The text is officially adopted at professional training courses held by Ing. Marco Gottardo at the classrooms of G-Tronic Robotics, in Padua. Compared to the previous edition it is enriched with new chapters for the design of sinusoidal oscillators, the analysis of the frequency response of higher-order active filters, waveform generators, noise analysis, hysteresis comparators, transistor interfacing for audio applications. An important chapter is dedicated to the introduction of the Eagle CAD for the design and development of printed circuits, with a clear guided example. Contains numerous exercises carried out SMD. Detailed chapter on analog filters. Great for self-taught and hobbyists

FPGA to High speed ADC Data streaming, HDL programming: Xilinx Zynq7000 family on Vivado IDE platform: Volume 1 (UK)

ISBN-10: 1720843694
ISBN-13: 978-1720843696

The book set the objective to design and test a high-speed and high-density data acquisition system based on the latest generation FPGA technologies. Topic is from the author Phd thesis and show the latest products released by Xilinx to design a acquire stream system of signals from generic probes (specifically magnetic probes apply on a nucler fusion experiment located in Padova, Italy). The Zynq 7000 family is nowadays state of the art of sistemy SoC that integrating a powerful and extensive FPGA section with an ARM mullticore, with the architecture Cortex A9. Inside the book the basis of HDL programming on Vivado IDE.

Let's program FPGA !!! First guided experience: FPGA Tutorial: Volume 1 (UK)
ISBN-10: 1720843694
ISBN-13: 978-1720843696
Amazon Prime

First chapter of a wide series of tutorials that introduce step by step to the last frontier of electronics. The SoC system with frontend in FPGA technology. Perfect for developing laboratory instruments including portable, robotics, civil and industrial controls, video processing systems and data streaming. To collect.